WATER-CONSERVING

Plants & Landscapes

FOR THE BAY AREA

PUBLISHED BY THE EAST BAY MUNICIPAL UTILITY DISTRICT

Principal Author and Technical Consultant

Barrie Coate

Acknowledgement

This book is a publication of the East Bay Municipal Utility District (EBMUD) as part of its water conservation program. Horticulturist Barrie Coate, as a consultant to the District, wrote most sections of this book and served as the primary source of technical material. The Administration Department's Water Conservation Unit coordinated the book assembly and reviews and supervised editing, design and production of this second edition.

Gayle Montgomery and Annette Oliveira, Public Information Office, edited and supervised design and production of the first edition. Linda Haymaker edited the second edition. David Kelsey, Manager of Public Information, edited the section on Water Efficient Irrigation and Water Conserving Grasses. Ali Harivandi wrote the section on Water Conserving Grasses and Chet Sarsfield wrote the section on Water Efficient Irrigation. Erika Aschmann, June Avila, Rick Hornbeck, and John Swindell reviewed the Plant, Landscape, and Irrigation section.

Technical Review

EBMUD appreciates the interest and assistance provided by the following individuals who reviewed the technical material as this book was being prepared:

Dave Amme, Horticulturist
Mai Arbegast, Landscape Architect
Russell Beatty, Landscape Architect
Don Brandeau, Landscape Architect
Barbara Coe, Nursery Manager
Charlie Danielsen, Horticulturist
Steve Edwards, Director, Tilden Botanic Garden
John Greenlee, Horticulturist
Peggy Grier, California Native Plant Society
Ali Harivandi, Turfgrass Consultant
Randall Ismay, Landscape Consultant
Antu Lucas, Bookbuyer, Magic Gardens
Ron Lutsko, Landscape Architect
John Meserve, Horticultural Consultant
Chris Pattillo, Landscape Architect
Wayne Roderick, Horticulturist
Jake Sigg, Strybing Arboretum
Jinks Tyler, Horticulturist
Ortha Zebroski, Landscape Architect

Illustration Credits

Cover photograph by Ali Davidson. Phillip Barker, Richard Bennett, John Blaustein, Barrie Coate, Carl Coate, Steve Edwards, Phillip Greig, Linda Haymaker, Ron Lutsko, Mike McKinley, Pam Peirce, Michael Thilgen, University of California, Berkeley, Department of Landscape Architecture and Ortho Books supplied all plant photographs. EBMUD appreciates the assistance of these individuals. EBMUD extends thanks to Sunset Books for allowing us to reproduce the San Francisco Bay Area climate zone map from the Sunset New Western Garden Book.

Table of Contents

Scope of the Book

Water conservation through landscaping offers the greatest single opportunity for water savings in the urban area. About 40 percent of urban water is used to irrigate gardens and lawns in California. Recent conversions of conventional landscapes (large percentage of lawn) into low-water-use landscapes—more appropriate to California's climate—show substantial water savings.

Homeowners and nursery/landscape professionals should consider ways to reduce water use of existing landscapes; to change existing landscapes so that they require modest watering; to plan new landscapes with low-water use as a major concern. A water-efficient landscape includes low-water-using plants, efficient irrigation systems and proper soil preparation.

Our wealth of plant material comes from all over the world. Mediterranean climates, like California's, offer water-conserving choices such as Eucalyptus from Australia, Escallonia from Chile, and Olive from Italy. Our California natives, which by definition are admirably suited to the sites where they grow, are also useful.

With water conservation as a prime consideration, it is still possible to design a balanced landscape. Lawns continue to serve a unique function and modest areas may be planted while maintaining an emphasis on water-conserving groundcovers, shrubs and trees. Low-water-use landscapes need not be dull—even in midsummer. Thoughtful selection of water-conserving plants can offer year-round interest with flowers, fruit, and foliage. A well-planned landscape, appropriate to California's climate, looks attractive and saves water, work, and money.

This book was designed as a reference on water-conserving plants. A long list of drought-tolerant plants was refined by subjecting each plant to a number of criteria. This book describes plants with the greatest potential for successful landscape performance.

The following criteria were used in the plant selection process:

Water Conserving

A water-conserving plant is one which requires less water than most others to grow well. This is quite relative since the water required varies between species and sites and can even be affected by microclimates and exposures within a particular garden.

The native plants from other countries which are best adapted to Mediterranean climates may be able to survive with no water other than available rainfall. This is rather restrictive; and although some plants selected for this list may need no supplemental water, the others will require no more than one deep watering during each of the dry months *once they have become established.*

It is not difficult to decrease landscape water use 50 percent by using low-water-requiring plants, reducing the amount of turf, changing water application from a time schedule to a need schedule, and applying water carefully to avoid runoff and evaporation.

Attractive Garden Plants

It is unnecessary to sacrifice an attractive landscape for the sake of water conservation. Many plants on this list, similar to those already in our gardens, provide lush foliage and flowers. In fact, many attractive plants in existing gardens are drought tolerant.

Generally Available in the Trade

If a recommended plant is not easy to obtain in the nursery trade, it is unlikely that the landscape designer, retail nursery or retail customer will wait for it. This list contains plants which are available from several growers, although not necessarily at all times.

Minimum Pest and Disease Problems

Most plants, including many listed here, have some insect and disease problems. These plants have been chosen because their problems do not require treatment or are less severe or more easily treated than some commonly used species. Many species have been omitted because of their history of insect, disease or soil type adaptation problems, or unacceptable amounts of limb breakage.

Require Little Pruning or Maintenance

Most plants should receive an annual cleanup and some light pruning. The shrubs and groundcovers in this list will perform beautifully with only light pruning in the spring. This should be done with hand shears, removing offending branches that protrude beyond the plant canopy. An annual spring slow-release fertilizer application would be adequate for most of these plants.

Compatibility with Sprinkler Water Systems

Most landscape installations are watered by sprinklers. This method of summer irrigation encourages root fungus diseases on many drought-tolerant plants. Of the plants that met all other criteria, those finally selected for this list (with a few noted exceptions) seem more tolerant of sprinkler irrigation.

California Landscapes—History

Given our Mediterranean climate (mild winters and dry summers), where did the overabundance of "thirsty" plants originate and how did they end up dominating today's ornamental landscape? Through the years, garden evolution has caused diversity to be the common denominator in our landscapes.

From the South. . .the first Franciscan missionaries tried planting California native plants along with those seeds brought in by sea trade. Those found to thrive in this hot, dry climate were planted in the mission courtyards. From these mission gardens were introduced the first plants to adorn homes and farms of the early settlers.

From the East. . .lush ornamental plants and New England lawns, which needed the year-round moisture found in the eastern U.S. to survive, first appeared in the West only where water from streams could support such vegetation. Only after irrigation technology and well drilling came into being did these gardens spread beyond immediate stream sides. The "newcomers" from the East were conquering the dry summer landscapes and replacing them with all the "comforts" of home.

It was soon found that nearly all plants could do well in the mild coastal California climate if water was available. With the development of the Central Valley Project, the Colorado River Aqueduct and the State Water Project, the floodgates were opened not only for a population boom but also for the production of ornamental plants and lawns. The California marketplace filled with plant material which had been the oddity only 50 years earlier. Even the landscape architect most compassionate to the semi-arid climate was frustrated when specifying drought-tolerant material because the plants were no longer available. The cycle began and most people in the industry slid into a "comfort zone". They regularly used water-loving exotics.

Note how the evolution of landscape design has revolved around water. During the 1976-1977 drought, tens of thousands of people in the Bay Area lost their landscapes at a cost that ran into the millions. Many of these people replaced their "thirsty" landscapes with drought-tolerant landscapes. An awareness of water shortfalls began and was strengthened by the reality of a growing population, rising energy costs and the variability of water supplies. A bold approach toward the production and use of appropriate plants is in order today as the evolutionary sequence of garden design carries us into tomorrow.

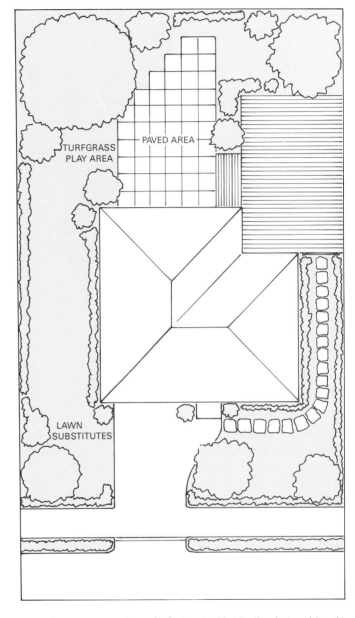

The modern water-conserving garden features "unthirsty" native plants and drought-resistant exotics and lawn substitutes. Areas formerly planted with turfgrass are now covered with decks and patios to minimize water use.

2

Planting Notes

Plant Sizes

Planting both a one- and a five-gallon container of the same species in the same site at the same time will usually provide surprising results. In three to five years, both plants will be the same size with the plant from the one gallon having produced more growth. In seven to ten years, the plant from the one gallon will be far more drought-tolerant and often larger than the one planted from the five gallon.

The faster growing the species is, the more pronounced this phenomenon seems to be. The younger plant produces a deeper, more widespread root system better enabling it to survive drought conditions and other stresses.

However, some slow-growing species are exceptions. If it is important to quickly produce a larger specimen in the landscape, the following species should be planted from five gallon or larger containers:

Ceratonia siliqua
Geijera parviflora
Ginkgo biloba cultivars
Lagerstroemia indica
Maytenus boaria
Meterosideros excelsus
Olea europa
Prunus lusitanica

Optimum Planting Season

The optimum season for planting in California is the cool season, fall through spring. Most woody plants (trees and shrubs) should be planted as early in fall as possible to insure good root establishment.

Winter rains, moderate temperatures, natural soil moisture, and growth cycle of the plant account for fall planting success. These factors cannot be replaced by simply providing irrigation to warm season planting.

Soil Tests

Planting may occur in less than optimum soils—those that have been excessively compacted during grading, areas with high mineral contents, or other problems. Condition of a soil may greatly affect the kinds of plants that will thrive there. Soil tests can describe the type of soil and its porosity, pH, fertility, salinity, mineral content, etc. Problems identified by soil testing can be efficiently corrected prior to planting to insure healthy growing conditions.

Soil samples are taken from the root zone of 3-4 locations. Varying depths may also be helpful if root development will be extending from shallow annuals to deep trees. Big sites with different exposures or problem spots can benefit from additional sampling.

Mulch

Mulching is an easy and very effective way to reduce the frequency of irrigation. Examples of organic mulch are leaves, bark, pine needles, chopped tree trimmings, etc. Rock and gravel are examples of inert mulches.

A 2-4" layer of organic mulch around trees, shrubs, and groundcovers can:

- Insulate the soil and roots from excessive drying.
- Reduce weeds.
- Add nutrients to the soil.
- Minimize compaction and erosion.

When mulching, do not cover the crown of the plant (where the trunk enters the ground). Instead, taper mulch to the crown at an angle. Do not use material from diseased plants.

Phased Planting

In nature, new soils and revegetating landscapes first support small plants, then increasingly larger ones. As the soil becomes enriched by ongoing plant debris, it provides for more growth and deeper root penetration. In new landscapes, groups of plants shelter one another from extremes of wind, cold, heat, and moisture loss.

On new and renewed sites, phase planting to make way for trees, shrubs and vines which take longer to establish. Underplant appropriate areas with short-term groundcovers, perennials, and annuals to provide attractive color the first few years, protect young trees and shrubs from extremes, and improve soil structure. As the larger or slower plants begin to grow and dominate, some underplantings can be phased out.

Soil Preparation
and CompGro™

Soil Preparation

A well-percolated soil is one which will absorb a water application of 1/2 inch or more per hour. Well-percolated soils are a must for most low-water-use plants which, as a group, grow poorly or die in water-logged soils. There can be several reasons for soils that absorb water poorly, and different remedies are needed for varying situations.

In level locations, frequently the problem is a subsurface hardpan which is impervious to water. The remedy is to break up the hardpan with deep ripping or by digging holes which penetrate the layer. Addition of a soil amendment then improves the soil structure and begins to promote good drainage and deep vigorous plant roots.

It is worth noting that the desirable "crumb" structure of the surface of most soils is very easily destroyed by the pounding of rain or sprinkler-applied water. The resulting formation is a compacted, slaked surface area with low capacity for water and air penetration—a formidable physical barrier to healthy root growth when dry. Mulches and drip irrigation minimize this problem.

Poor percolation can also occur in a tightly packed clay topsoil. This condition may be improved by the addition of gypsum and quantities of organic material like fir bark mulch, compost, or CompGro™. These materials must be incorporated as deeply as possible; a minimum of 8 inches for perennials.

Poorly percolated soils high in silt present a different problem. Their structure cannot be stabilized as can that of clay soils so large amounts (25 percent and more) of a relatively inert organic material such as redwood sawdust or chipped bark are frequently incorporated into them to change their physical characteristics enough to allow good drainage.

Sandy soils percolate excessively and present a problem in that they contain only a small amount of usable water per foot of depth. Since plants root more deeply in sandy soils, the water available to the plants is not necessarily too different from that of other well-percolated soils. The water-holding capacity of a sandy soil also can be increased by adding organic material.

In other details of soil preparation, such as fertilization and acidification, low-water-using plants vary in their needs. The charts beginning on page 21 will serve as a guide.

CompGro™

"CompGro™" contains one of the by-products of the wastewater treatment process and is produced by the East Bay Municipal Utility District. CompGro™ is a natural, humuslike compost that looks and feels like soil. It is not soil, but an amendment that increases your soil's organic content and water retention ability. It also provides some necessary nutrients (nitrogen, phosphorus, and potassium) and valuable trace elements such as zinc. Use of CompGro™ for leafy vegetables and other food chain crops intended for direct human consumption is not recommended.

What does CompGro™ do?
•Enriches soil with nitrogen and vital nutrients
•Improves water retention and absorption
•Allows air and water to penetrate the soil
•Promotes faster root development and reduces transplant shock
•Buffers soil against abrupt pH changes
•Decreases density of compacted soil

How much CompGro™ should I use?

Lawn Planting: Blend two to four two-cubic-foot bags of CompGro™ into the top four to six inches of soil for each 100 square feet. If your soil is hard or infertile, use the higher rate.

Planting Shrubs and Trees: Uniformly blend one part CompGro™ with three parts soil in the planting hole. Use three shovelfuls for each five-gallon plant and one shovelful for each one-gallon plant.

Top Dressing Lawns (New Lawns or Existing Lawns): Spread or broadcast one bag per each 200 square feet after seeding and again each spring and fall for a healthy, vigorous lawn.

Flowers, Bulbs and Color Plantings: Mix one bag of CompGro™ into the soil for six bedding plant packs (12 to 25 square feet) or use one shovelful for each plant or bulb.

Ground Covers: Mix one bag of CompGro™ into the soil for each flat of ground cover (50 square feet) or use a heaping handful mixed into the soil for each plant.

Mulching Garden Areas: Apply a one-inch layer of CompGro™ to flower and shrub beds (use one bag for each 25 square feet).

Potting Mixes: Mix one part CompGro™ with equal parts of sand and redwood sawdust or combine one part CompGro™ with two parts of a good commercial potting soil.

Water Efficient Irrigation

Irrigation is needed for the majority of California's landscapes. Our limited water resources require us to approach irrigation design with water efficiency in mind.

Irrigation equipment is available for every type of application: overhead spray, misting, flooding, and drip. By using it properly, high water efficiency can be achieved.

The variety of irrigation equipment available can cause considerable confusion. Irrigation components necessary for an efficient and properly designed irrigation system are discussed below.

Automatic Controllers

A flexible and reliable irrigation controller is a primary tool for water conserving irrigation. Controllers should be solid state for more accurate timing to allow for shorter watering cycles. Several important features should be considered when choosing a controller:

•**Multiple program capability** gives you the option to water different areas according to their needs. Some areas may need to be irrigated three times a week, while other areas may need water only once a week.

•**Calendar-program flexibility** is determined by the number of days in the program. Most controllers operate on a 7 or 14-day calendar. A longer calendar program will provide greater flexibility in programming for various application needs and will be more adaptable to potential restrictions such as even or odd-day watering regulations.

•**Multiple repeat cycle capabilities** is an extremely important feature for minimizing runoff, especially when watering planted slopes with clay soils. Multiple repeat cycling allows you to divide one long irrigation period into a series of shorter irrigation periods with time in between to allow the water to soak into the ground. For instance, a 15-minute application can be divided into three 5-minute cycles with an hour in between each cycle.

Carefully analyze your landscape, your irrigation system, and your programming needs. Then invest in a controller that will meet all of those needs.

Remote Control Valves

Remote control valves regulate the flow of water to the plants in your landscape. Each valve controls a separate section of the irrigation system and allows for different areas to be watered independently.

Many remote control valves are now made of molded plastic, are non-corroding, easy to work with, and less expensive than metal valves.

Some incorporate pressure regulators to maintain a constant reduced pressure for best operation of the equipment in a given landscape section. Some are designed to operate on very low flows for control of drip irrigation systems or sections. Shop for the special valve features needed for best control of your system.

Sprinklers

Two basic types of sprinkler heads are used in irrigation systems: spray heads and rotors. Spray heads emit a fixed, solid canopy of spray over the area covered. Rotor heads are those with a rotating nozzle that turn slowly to distribute water in moving streams over the area. Both types are available in a variety of coverage patterns.

Spray heads usually have a smaller distribution pattern than rotors and are better suited for use in small areas. Rotor heads throw water further and higher and are, therefore, better suited for large open areas.

Spray and rotor heads are available in pop-up models for use in lawn, shrub, and groundcover areas.

Application Rates, Patterns and Spacings

One of the most important points in selecting sprinkler heads of either type is to make sure that the sprinklers which will operate together have matching, or at least compatible, application rates. This means that if a full-circle spray head discharges 4 gallons per minute (gpm), a matching half-circle must discharge 2 gpm and a quarter-circle 1 gpm. This applies to sprinklers with the same radius of throw. Most spray heads will have matching or compatible precipitation rates while many rotor heads will not.

Most sprinkler heads have a distribution pattern that places more water close to the head and less toward the outer edge of the coverage area. The spray patterns must overlap to level out this distribution, usually throwing from head to head (50% of diameter spacing).

For proper distribution, operating pressure at the sprinkler must be in the range recommended by the manufacturer.

Choose sprinklers carefully according to the area and the use. Space them correctly for proper overlap; you don't want to overwater 90 percent of the area because of poor coverage in the other 10 percent. If wind is a problem, use low trajectory nozzles to minimize waste and improve distribution. Keep in mind that nozzles with different performances are interchangeable in most sprinkler heads so corrective adjustments can be made after the sprinklers have been installed.

Drip and Micro Irrigation

Drip and micro irrigation are methods of delivering water to selected plants in a slow, precise manner. When small emitters, perforated tube or porous tube are used, the system is usually called drip. When extremely small sprinklers and misters are used, they are often referred to as micro irrigation. Both operate on very low flows measured in gallons per hour (gph) instead of gallons per minute (gpm). They may generally be mixed in a single section or system.

Drip irrigation is an excellent tool for water conservation. Emitters, drip tubing or soaker tubing all place water on the surface of the soil. There is little water loss due to evaporation. Application is so slow, at 1/2 to about 4 gph, that there is little or no runoff or puddling. Since emitter rates vary in increments of 1/2 to 1 gph, they can easily be changed to adjust the amount of water to a particular plant or pot. A large plant or tree can be supplied by using multiple emitters or a loop of drip tubing. Tiny plants, tubs and hanging pots can be irrigated efficiently by adding, changing or eliminating emitters as needed. Probably the greatest conservation factor is that water is applied only to a plant's root zone and not to bare ground or weeds.

Drip irrigation equipment can operate on either low or high pressures. A pressure regulator at the connection to a low pressure system is necessary for even flows. High pressure drip systems can now be retrofitted to existing sprinkler systems.

Since low flow rates are controlled by very small orifices in emitters and micro-sprinklers, fine filters are also required to avoid clogging of virtually all drip systems. Be sure that the proper filter and pressure regulator are installed.

Flexible polyethylene tubing is the standard water supply line in drip irrigation systems. Sizes are generally quite small since 1/2" tube is rated at up to 320 gph and 1/8" tube to 4 gph. Emitters, drip lines, and soakers are normally laid on top of the ground and covered with bark or mulch. Micro and mini sprinklers are positioned on plastic or metal stakes just above the foliage of ground-covers or other plants. Either system can be easily moved for maintenance or repositioned for changes in plantings.

Use pressure-compensating emitters if there are elevation differences of more than a few feet in the area to be drip irrigated. Standard emitters will discharge more water from the lower emitters and less from the higher, so irrigation won't be uniform.

A word of caution concerning drip irrigation systems. Pre-packaged drip irrigation systems generally have inexpensive components which can lead to clogging, uneven flows and other problems. These systems rarely contain either the proper components or the proper number of components to perform the installation correctly. Contact an irrigation supply outlet or irrigation design specialist before purchasing drip irrigation equipment.

Special Conservation Devices

The following devices can improve irrigation efficiency:

Check valves are designed to stop drainage through sprinkler heads. When installed under the heads, they will stop pipes from draining after each use, eliminating both water waste and soggy spots around low heads.

A **rain switch** is a very simple conservation device. It is placed in an open area out of range of sprinklers. It consists of a container to catch rain and a switch wired to the controller that will shut off sprinkler operation when a pre-set amount of rain has fallen. It eliminates the waste and embarrassment of running sprinklers in the rain.

Irrigation System Design

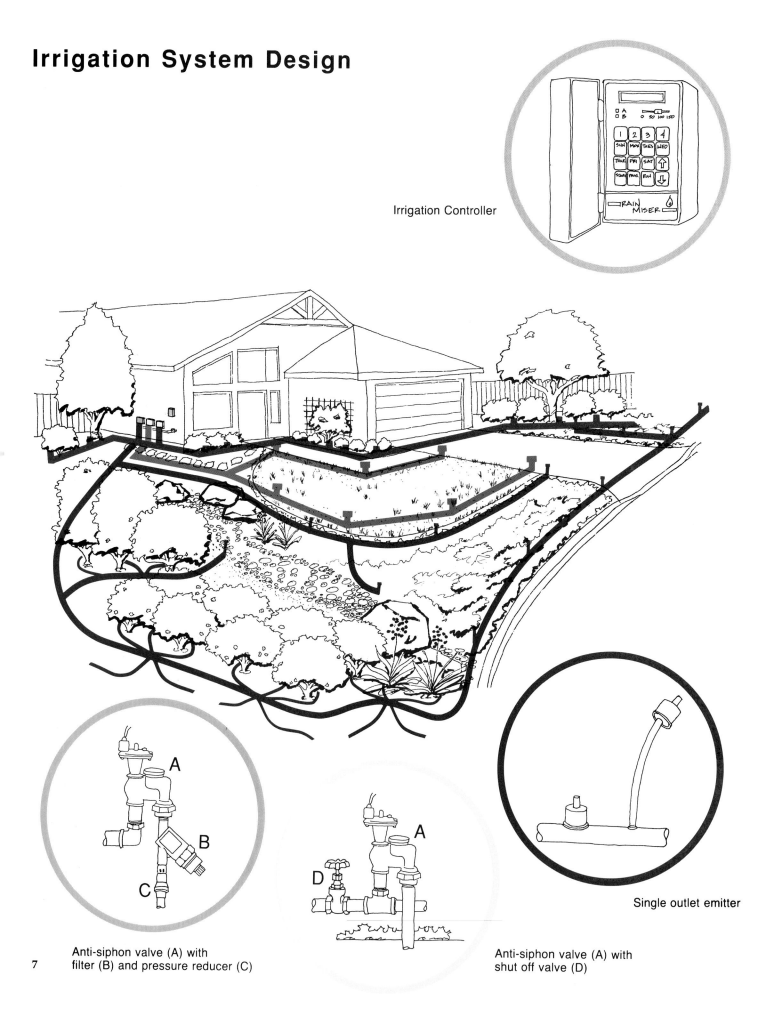

Irrigation Controller

Anti-siphon valve (A) with
filter (B) and pressure reducer (C)

Anti-siphon valve (A) with
shut off valve (D)

Single outlet emitter

Irrigation Equipment

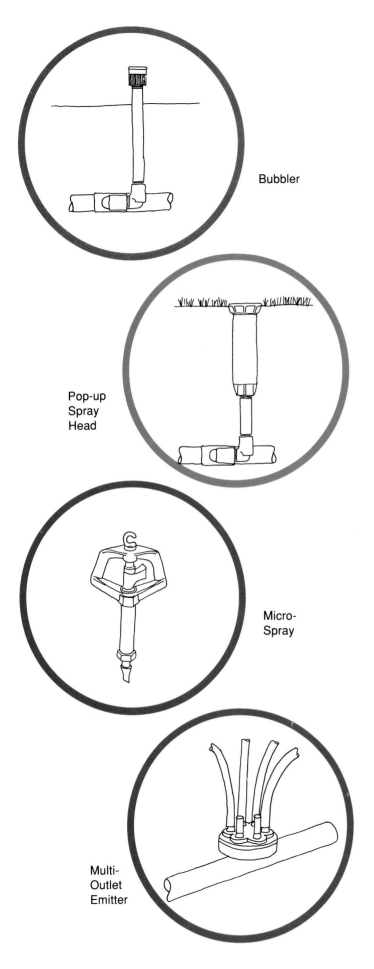

Bubbler

Pop-up
Spray
Head

Micro-
Spray

Multi-
Outlet
Emitter

The key to an efficient irrigation system is to use the proper equipment in the right place. By doing so, you can insure that the water you apply is being used by the plants, not being wasted.

The landscape on the left employs three different kinds of irrigation. The *red* system running along the house is a high-pressure bubbler. The *green* system irrigating the lawn is a high-pressure system of matched precipitation rate pop-up spray heads. The *blue* system in the foreground is a micro-irrigation drip system requiring low pressure.

All three systems use electric remote control valves to control the flow of water into the lateral lines. In addition, an anti-siphon valve is attached to each of the three systems to prevent the irrigation water from being drawn back into the potable water supply used indoors.

The micro-irrigation system (*blue*) requires two extra components in addition to the anti-siphon valve. Since micro-irrigation systems are designed to work at low pressure, a regulator is used to reduce the pressure to 15 to 25 PSI. A filter is also needed to keep debris from entering the system and clogging the emitters.

Three types of micro-irrigation devices are shown at left. They are single emitters, multiple emitters and microsprays. A single emitter applies precise amounts of water to the base of one plant. Multiple emitters can apply water at up to six points. Microspray emitters deliver either fine sprays or jets of water at very low rates. Together, micro-irrigation devices can create a very efficient water delivery system.

The entire irrigation system is operated by the irrigation controller, shown at the left in *light blue*, which electrically opens and closes the valves. To keep the system efficient, the controller must be reprogrammed periodically to match seasonal weather changes.

Basics of Installing Drip Irrigation

Most low-pressure drip systems should include:

- •anti-siphon valves
- •filters
- •pressure reducers or pressure regulators
- •distribution line, 1/2" flexible polyethylene tubing
- •micro tubing, 1/4" flexible polyethylene tubing
- •connecting fittings, tees, elbows, couplers, etc.
- •single and multiple outlet drip emitters
- •microsprays or microjets

Before starting installation, check with local authorities to determine requirements for backflow prevention devices or anti-siphon valves. These devices prevent irrigation water from mixing with the potable drinking water supply.

Drip or micro irrigation is usually installed after plant placement.

Lay out your site on paper. Show buildings, paving, plants, and the location of your water source. Segregate the plants into zones of low, medium, or high water use. Decide where to locate valves and what type of microspray or drip emitters are needed. Descriptions of components are listed in manufacturers' catalogs, which are available free from local irrigation suppliers. Once your design is complete, you are ready to start.

A shutoff valve should be installed between the water source and the irrigation system to allow repair of the system without disrupting inside use.

To operate properly, anti-siphon valves must be installed 12" above the highest sprinkler or emitter. Separate valves are needed for each area with different water use requirements. A filter is required after the valve to keep the small sprays and emitters from clogging.

Most drip and microspray products are designed to be used with water pressures between 15 and 25 PSI. Therefore, a pressure reducer must be installed after the filter to insure precise delivery rates and to prevent non-glued compression fittings from separating. Make sure the arrows on all valves and pressure reducers point in the direction of water flow.

Drip or "poly" tubing can either be placed on top of the soil and covered with mulch or buried in shallow trenches. A four-inch

Emitter Selection Guidelines

Plant Material	# Of Emitters	Flow Rate	Placement
Small Shrubs	1	1gph	At Root Zone
Medium Shrubs	2	1gph	Space evenly in Root Zone
Large Shrubs	3	2gph	Space evenly in Root Zone
Small Trees	2	2gph	Space evenly in Root Zone
Large Trees	4+	2gph	Space evenly in Root Zone
Groundcover	Perforated or Porous tubing	Varies	Run parallel lines 12-18" apart

trench is deep enough to keep usual garden tools from harming the tubing. Dig trenches between two rows of plants. Connect the 1/2" poly tubing to the pressure reducer and lay it in the trench, pinning it down between plants. The poly tubing is flexible to weave through the garden as needed; however, there are also connecting tees and elbows available.

Flush the system. Connect the 1/4" micro-tubing to the 1/2" poly line using a proper hole punch. Run the 1/4" tubing to the base of each plant. Leave a few inches of 1/4" tubing above the soil; emitters will be attached here finally. If the site is not flat, locate the emitters on the uphill side of the plants. Check and adjust all microsprays and emitters for proper flow and coverage.

Irrigation Scheduling

Establishment Period

Water-conserving plants must be watered similarly to other plants until they become well rooted. Young plants are fully dependent on the water supplied directly to the root ball. For the first growing season, water at regular intervals in a containment basin the same diameter as the root ball.

Most plants will be well established after one full year, and thereafter will need thorough watering only once or twice a month during the summer. This compares with the need to water turf landscapes every three days.

Evapotranspiration (ET)

Evapotranspiration, or ET for short, is used to describe a plant's water needs. ET is a measure of the amount of water that has evaporated from the soil and transpired through the leaves of a plant. The amount of water that transpires through the leaves of a plant varies from plant to plant.

EBMUD operates a weather station that develops ET information for lawns. The chart below shows lawn water needs in inches of water required per month. The solid line represents inland water requirements and the dashed line costal water requirements. In the inland regions in July, lawns require about 7 inches of water. In the winter, however, lawns require almost no supplemental water because precipitation usually exceeds ET.

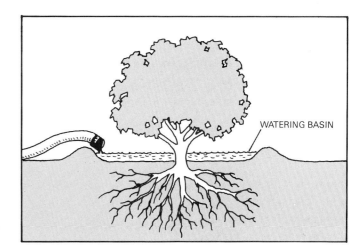

WATERING BASIN

Using a watering basin the same diameter as the root ball will help to establish deep, healthy roots. Extensive rooting will be encouraged by slow, low-volume watering such as that provided by drip irrigation.

Annually, lawn requires about 40 inches of water in inland areas and 25 inches of water in coastal areas. Generally, water-conserving plants require less than half the water of lawn.

Watering Method

Irrigate when first signs of wilt occur or when a moisture meter reads in the "dry" range. Irrigate thoroughly to get water deep to the roots. If in doubt about the depth of moisture penetration, use a moisture meter or dig into the soil.

Irrigate in the early morning when wind and evaporation are least. Use short, repeat cycles to avoid runoff or puddling.

Use common sense. Check soil moisture frequently, and adjust irrigation programs for the weather, the seasons, and the plant's needs.

System Inspection

Frequently observe your irrigation system in operation, preferably weekly. Trim grass or foliage blocking spray heads. Immediately repair broken or leaking sprinklers, risers, and valves. Make sure part-circle sprinklers are adjusted not to spray on pavement.

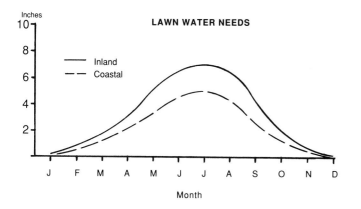

Erosion Control and Fire-Retardant Plants

Plants for Erosion Control—Successful erosion control requires some basic understanding of the forces involved when earth movement occurs. Landscape irrigation of a slope is equivalent to 25 to 60 inches of rainfall per year. Overwatering, the cause of many slope failures, can equal 100 inches of rainfall per year when winter rains are added. High volumes of water, added to slopes that have evolved and stabilized in a climate of 20 to 30 inches of rain per year, can seriously reduce slope stability.

The most common undesirable soil movement is a surface slip which finds a shallow but wide section of surface soil sliding off the subsoil, carrying all vegetation with it. Decreasing this type of problem requires the use of such deep-rooted plants as African Sumac, Oleander or Carob Tree, while the surface soil is held in place by groundcovers like *Coprosma kirkii*, *Cotoneaster congestus* 'Likiang' or *Arctotheca calendula*—Cape Weed. *Carpobrotus edulis*—African Ice Plant, should not be used to prevent soil erosion. Its foliage is so heavy that it can pull down a bank of wet soil.

Covering the steepest slopes with jute netting through which plants may be installed is an added precaution.

Trees
Aesculus californica—California Buckeye
Agonis flexuosa—Peppermint Tree
Celtis species—Hackberry
Ceratonia siliqua—Carob Tree
Cercis species—Redbud
Eucalyptus species
Pistacia chinensis—Chinese Pistache
Quercus species—Oak
Shrubs
Ceanothus species—California Lilac
Cistus species—Rockrose
Cotoneaster species
Eriogonum species—Buckwheat
Lavandula species—Lavender

Leonotis leonurus—Lion's Tail
Mahonia species—Holly Grape
Myrsine africana—African Box
Rhus integrifolia—Lemonade Berry
Ribes viburnifolium—Evergreen Currant
Xylosma congestum—Shiny Xylosma
Vines
Cissus antarctica—Kangaroo Ivy
Euonymous fortunei—Winter Creeper
Rosa banksiae—Lady Banks Rose
Vitus vinifera—Grape
Groundcovers
Acacia redolens
Arctostaphylos species—Manzanita

Baccharis pilularis—Dwarf Coyote Bush
Ceanothus species—California Lilac
Coprosma species
Gazania species
Hypericum calycinum—St. John's Wort
Juniperus species—Juniper
Lantana montevidensis
Myoporum 'Pacificum'
Rosmarinus officinalis cultivars—Rosemary
Delosperma species ⎫
Drosanthemum species ⎬ Ice Plant
Lampranthus species ⎪
Malephora species ⎭

Fire-Retardant Plants—A fire-retardant landscape is created partly by using plants which are less flammable and partly by wise placement and arrangement of plants. Several rules should be followed to prevent a brush or range fire from destroying a home.

First, a 50-foot band of fire-retardant plants should be used around structures, especially in hilly areas. Second, within 50 feet of structures, medium-sized shrubs should not be used beneath the canopies of trees. These tend to create a "fire ladder" into the tree from which flames can jump or be blown. Third, large trees should not be planted so that their foliage will be within 10 feet of any structure. Fourth, keep dry grass mowed, remove all dead wood, and remove heavy tree litter within 100 feet of structures and from beneath shrubs. Fifth, highly flammable trees such as pines and eucalyptus (all species) should not be planted near buildings; but if they are, the lower limbs should be removed to reduce "fire ladder" potential. No clear-cut definition of relative fire retardation in plants has been defined, but the plants in the list offered below are far more retardant than most.

An additional worthwhile device is an irrigation line supplying sprinklers which wet down surrounding vegetation in an emergency. They can be operated from a single manual valve.

Trees
Arbutus unedo—Strawberry Tree
Ceratonia siliqua—Carob Tree
Cercis occidentalis—Redbud
Rhus lancea—African Sumac
Shrubs
Cistus species—Rockrose
Heteromeles arbutifolia—Toyon
Nerium oleander—Oleander
Prunus ilicifolia—Holly-Leaved Cherry
Prunus lyonii—Catalina Cherry
Rhamnus californica—Coffeeberry

Rhus integrifolia—Lemonade Berry
Vines
Solanum jasminoides—Potato Vine
Tecomaria capensis—Cape Honeysuckle
Trachelospermum jasminoides—Star Jasmine
Groundcovers
Aloe species
Arctotheca calendula—Cape Weed
Delosperma alba—Ice Plant
Drosanthemum floribundum—Ice Plant
Duchesnea indica—Mock Strawberry

Fragaria chiloensis—Wild Strawberry
Lampranthus species—Ice Plant
Melephora crocea—Ice Plant
Rosmarinus officinalis prostrata—Prostrate Rosemary
Perennials
Achillea tomentosa—Woolly Yarrow
Agapanthus—Lily of the Nile
Diplacus—Monkey Flower
Santolina species—Lavender Cotton
Tricostemma lanatum—Woolly Blue Curls

Water Conserving Grasses and Lawn Substitutes

Turfgrass has many practical applications in the urban setting including use for:

- recreation
- erosion control
- temperature modification
- glare reduction
- aesthetic effects
- control of dust and mud

However, the usefulness of turfgrass is tempered by its water consumption. A significant portion of urban water use is for lawn irrigation.

The following guidelines should be followed when using turfgrass:

- Use turf only when functionally required.
- Use drought tolerant species.
- Prepare soil properly for lawn sod or seed.
- Use nitrogen fertilizer sparingly in summer.
- Aerate or topdress compacted lawns in heavy clay soils at least annually to improve water penetration.
- Remove thatch buildup annually.

Several turfgrasses adapted to the San Francisco Bay Area exhibit superior drought tolerance. The reader is encouraged to review all pertinent characteristics of these grasses before selecting one. All other variables being equal, the following turfgrasses may need 10-20% less water than lawns of bluegrass or mixed bluegrass-perennial ryegrass.

Bermudagrass (Cynodon spp.)

Bermudagrass, a perennial warm-season turfgrass, is grown extensively in California's semi-tropical regions from the Mexican border to the north end of the Sacramento Valley. It is also grown in the moderate climates of California coastal regions including the San Francisco Bay Area. Common bermudagrass (*Cynodon dactylon*), is grown from seed, but the most widely used bermudagrasses in recent years are vegetatively propagated, hybrid varieties like 'Santa Ana', 'Tifway', and 'Tifgreen'.

All bermudagrasses become dormant if grown where winter soil temperatures drop below 50-55°F. Thus, in the San Francisco Bay Area, these grasses may remain dormant for up to four months depending on variety and location. When dormant during the winter, bermudagrass shoots and roots stop growing and appear dead. If the straw color of dormant bermudagrass is objectionable, overseeding with a cool-season grass such as perennial ryegrass can provide winter color.

Bermudagrass is both a low-water and low-maintenance turfgrass. It has excellent heat, drought and salt tolerance. Disadvantages of both common and hybrid bermudagrasses are a lack of shade tolerance and an invasive nature. They invade adjacent planting areas quickly, and eradicating the bermudagrass may take several months and require the use of herbicides.

Hybrid Bermudagrass (Cynodon spp.)

Common Bermudagrass (Cynodon dactylon)

Water Conserving Grasses and Lawn Substitutes

Tall Fescue (Festuca arundinacea)

The new turf-type tall fescues have nearly the leaf width and dark green color of bluegrass, and can make a beautiful lawn.

A cool-season grass, tall fescue stays green all year and is well adapted to the San Francisco Bay Area. It has a dense and extensive root system, concentrated in the top 12 inches of soil. Its roots can, however, penetrate to four feet in deep soils where less frequent but deep irrigation is practiced. Deep rooting enhances tall fescue's ability to survive prolonged drought and/or infrequent irrigation.

Tall fescue is established from seed or sod. A seeding rate of 10 pounds per 1,000 square feet is recommended. The recommended mowing height for tall fescue is 1-1/2 to 3 inches. Since tall fescue does not produce runners, it will not invade adjacent plantings. Tall fescue varieties suitable for the Bay Area include 'Jaguar', 'Olympic', 'Adventure', 'Apache', 'Falcon', 'Mustang', 'Houndog', 'Maverick', and 'Tempo'.

Tall Fescue (Festuca arundinacea)

Hard Fescue (Festuca longifolia)

Hard fescue is a medium-tall, long-lived, densely tufted, non-creeping bunch-type grass. Leaf texture is very fine. Its root system penetrates quite deeply, contributing to its high drought tolerance. A heavy root system plus abundant, dense leaves and a low crown make hard fescue an excellent grass for erosion control.

It is adapted to mowing; however, *it is not recommended as mowed turf in areas with hot summers, such as the inland areas of the San Francisco Bay Region.* Unmowed hard fescue is an attractive groundcover with a natural, meadowy appearance. It does well in poor soils and in shaded areas.

Hard fescue is a prime candidate for low-maintenance and nonused areas of home landscape, median strips, golf course roughs, parks, and cemetaries. Drooping leaves not more than 12 inches long and thinned seed heads make it an attractive groundcover. Since leaves stay green year-round, hard fescue is not a fire hazard. If green color is desired, however, some summer irrigation is essential. If not irrigated in the summer, the grass will be dormant and may become a fire hazard. Among commonly used hard fescue varieties are 'Scaldis', 'Tournament', and 'Aurora'.

Hard Fescue (Festuca longifolia)

Water Conserving Grasses and Lawn Substitutes

Lawn Substitutes

If grass is not required, other plants which require little water and will accept occasional foot traffic are:

Achillea tomentosa - Woolly Yarrow
Plant 2-1/4 inch pots six inches apart, mow in March and July to a height of 2 inches.

Thymus herba-barona - Caraway-Scented Thyme
Plant all Thymes from 2-1/4 inch pots six to eight inches apart. Mowing not necessary. Rose-pink flowers cover the plant in early summer. Attracts bees in summer.

Thymus praecox-arcticus - Mother of Thyme
2 to 6 inches tall, purple and white flowers. Mow to 1-1/2 inches in July and fertilize. Attracts bees in summer.

Trifolium fragiferum - O'Connor's Legume
Plant from seed in fall. Mow to 2 inches in April, June, August. Attracts bees in summer.

Sprinklers may be used on all these plants, presuming soil is prepared as for lawn planting, but frequency of watering should be reduced to conform to the species' needs.

Ornamental Grasses

Many ornamental grasses are now being used for their ease of cultivation, drought tolerance and attractiveness. Page 83 describes ornamental grasses that are perennial and clumping with deep root systems that resist dry extremes. They are useful in mixed borders and shrubberies or when massed, to create a meadow effect as an alternative to a high water-use lawn. Native bunch grasses are forgiving of poor soils, and can grow well at garden edges, hillsides, banks and other dry spots. Since ornamental grasses are relatively new to nurseries, and very popular, many new varieties continue to appear on the market. Ask your grower about recommendations for your area. Many grasses can also be bought by seed or ordered through the mail. (See lists of availability in Resource Section.)

Drought Tolerant Turfgrass Characteristics for the San Francisco Bay Area

	Tall Fescue *Festuca arundinacea*	Hard Fescue *Festuca longifolia*	Hybrid Bermudagrass *Cynodon spp.*	Common Bermudagrass *Cynodon dactylon*
Texture (Leaf Blade Width)	C	Fi	M	C
Growth Habit	B	B	R-S	R-S
Establishment Method	Se	Se	So/St	Se/St
Establishment Rate	F	M	F	F
Growth Rate	F	M	F	F
Winter Color	G	G	D	D
Cutting Height (inches)	1.5-3	NM or 1.5-2.5 (in shade)	0.5-1.0	0.5-1.5
Drought Tolerance	M	M	H	H
Heat Tolerance	M	L	H	H
Shade Tolerance	H	VH	L	L
Nitrogen Requirements	M	L	H	L
Dethatching Needs	L	L	H	H
Wear Tolerance	H	M	H	H
Salinity Tolerance	M	L	H	H
Weed Invasion	L	M	L	L
Disease Incidence	L	H	L	L

Key to the Table

B - Bunch type (non creeper)
C - Coarse (wide leaf blades)
D - Dormant (straw color)
F - Fast
Fi - Fine (narrow leaf blades)
G - Green
H - High
L - Low
M - Medium
NM - Non-mowed (groundcover)
R - Rhizome (creeper)
S - Stolon (creeper)
Se - Seeded
So - Sodded
St - Stolonized (sprigged)
VH - Very high

Definition of Terms on Chart

The meaning of some of the terms in the charts opposite the plant photos is apparent while others deserve explanation. CULTURAL PREFERENCES are separated from CULTURAL TOLERANCES to emphasize that the conditions a plant prefers and the conditions it tolerates may be different. For example, Black Walnut prefers irrigation, but will tolerate a waterless environment.

"CN" under the numerical listing for a plant indicates that it is a California Native.

Important Characteristics
GROWTH RATES are defined as VF (Very Fast), F (Fast), M (Moderate), and S (Slow). In trees, Fast growth would be typified by Aleppo Pine, at 2' or more per year, while Slow to Moderate growth would be typified by Swamp Myrtle, at 8" per year. In shrubs, Fast growth might be seen in Red Clusterberry at 2-3' per year for several years, while Slow growth might be typified by Portugal Laurel at 3-6" per year.

Black circles (•) on the chart in the categories listed below mean that a plant displays the indicated characteristics.

Cultural Preferences
Plants preferring GOOD DRAINAGE should not be planted in unmodified, heavy clay soils. Many of the species on this list prefer soil which drains rapidly and resent excessive moisture retained around their root collar or root tips.

Plants which prefer to be watered regularly on a permanent basis are indicated in the IRRIGATION column. "Regular watering" refers to one application during each of the hottest six months of the year. Even the plants on this list which will survive with no summer watering will look better if they receive this monthly supplement.

Cultural Tolerances
The NO WATER column identifies plants which will perform well even in the interior valley with no irrigation once they are established.

The ALKALINE SOIL column is primarily used to identify plants which perform satisfactorily in soils laden with excessive levels of calcium and magnesium. Some of these plants are tolerant of high sodium levels as well. Alkaline soils commonly have pH levels of eight to nine. Many also contain a high proportion of fine clay particles which create a very dense soil structure accentuating the problem created by the high pH levels.

The SEACOAST CONDITIONS column can be used to select plants which perform well within 1,000 feet of the ocean or bay. Most of these plants tolerate some amount of salt air and wind, usually becoming more densely foliaged than in inland gardens and developing more intense flower colors.

The SPRINKLERS column provides guidance in the selection of water-conserving plants which will perform satisfactorily in the existing landscape that receives sprinkler irrigation. As an example, a water-conserving groundcover such as Coprosma 'Verde Vista' could replace a lawn surrounded by Junipers and watered by impulse sprinklers. The sprinklers may be retained and used on a drastically reduced schedule to the benefit of the Junipers and the water bill. When new or retrofitted landscape installations are planned, the use of bubbler or low-volume irrigation should be considered. Plants prefer the deep watering pro-vided and the water savings are substantial using this technique.

A circle in the WIND column means that the plant *will* tolerate winds of ten miles per hour or more. Consistent winds occur in many sites including the seashore and "wind tunnel" streets in many cities. Many Zone 15 gardens suffer from a strong, warm wind in the afternoon. Many water-conserving plants, like Forget-Me-Nots, do not tolerate 10 mph winds.

Absence of a circle in the HEAT column means a plant does not tolerate heat well and should be used only in north, east, or heavily shaded locations. A plant's tolerance of heat should not be confused with its preference for sun. Although almost all of the plants on this list tolerate HEAT, many prefer partial shade, particularly in the very hottest locations.

Sunset Climate Zones: The *Sunset Western Garden Book* defines climate zones in the Bay Area based on elevation, influence of the Pacific Ocean, presence of hills and other factors. Numbers in the SUNSET ZONES column show the zones where a plant will succeed best. The map opposite this page shows where these zones are located. In the Bay Area, the Concord-Walnut Creek area is typical of Zone 14; the Berkeley hills of Zone 16, the areas near the water, of Zone 17.

Aesthetic and Cultural Compatibility: Numbers in this column correspond with selected plants from the list which are suggested as companions. These are not comprehensive lists of plant combinations, merely suggestions to stimulate the design process. The combinations should be visually pleasing while performing well together with the same exposure and watering program.

Sunset Climate Zones

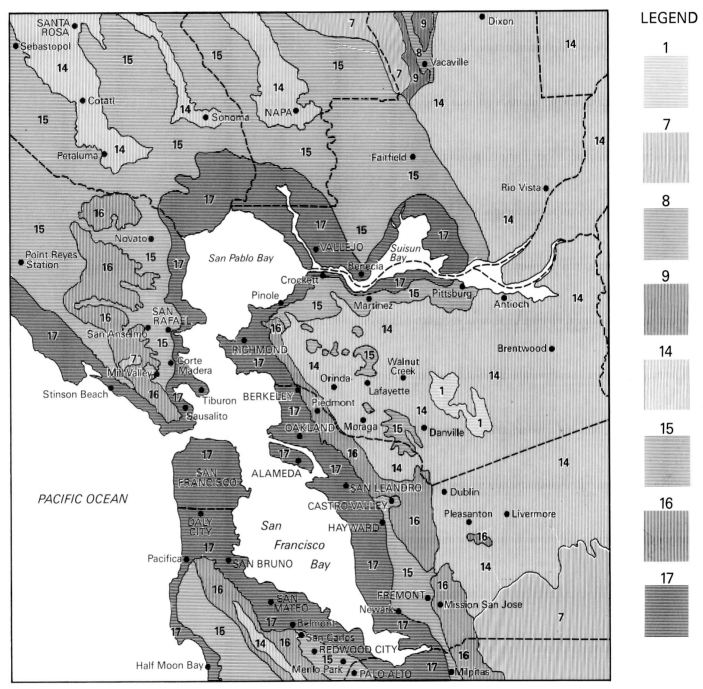

Bay Area climate zones ranging from semi-arid (7) to coastal (17) are noted in charts beginning on page 21.

Plant Index—
Common Names

TS1	Abelia, Glossy	TS63	Cherry, Hollyleaf, Catalina	P41	Geranium, Common
T1	Acacia, Bailey	T66	Chinese Date	P27	Geranium, Trailing
T4	Alder, Italian	T63	Chinese Scholar Tree	GC32	Germander
P5	Aloe	T38	Christmas Tree, New Zealand	P57	Germander, Bush
P11	Alyssum, Perennial	V4	Clematis, Evergreen	AB4	Godetia
AB13	Alyssum, Sweet	TS21	Clusterberry, Red	T31	Goldenrain Tree
TS10	Anemone, Bush	TS66	Coffeeberry, California	TS71	Gooseberry, Fuchsia-Flowered
P7	Artemisia, Silver Mound	T22	Coolibah Tree	V23	Grape
T26	Ash, Evergreen	GC16	Coprosma, Creeping	OG2	Grass, Blue Oat
T24	Ash, Moraine	GC17	Coprosma, Verde Vista	OG4	Grass, Deer
T25	Ash, Raywood	AB6	Coreopsis	OG5	Grass, Fountain
P10	Aubretia, Common	AB7	Cosmos	OG6	Grass, Needle
AB3	Bachelor's Button	AB8	Cosmos, Yellow	OG3	Grass, Zebra
TS57	Bamboo, Golden	SS5	Cotoneaster, Likiang	TS33	Grevillea, Canberra
SS14	Bamboo, Heavenly	T50	Cottonwood, Nevada Male	TS34	Grevillea, Rosemary
TS6	Barberry, Darwin's	GC6	Coyote Brush, Dwarf	SS10	Grevillea, Woolly
TS7	Barberry, Japanese	T34	Crabapple, Robinson	TS29	Guava, Pineapple
P1	Bear's Breech	P26	Cranesbill	V10	Guinea Gold Vine
P42	Bearded Tongue	T32	Crape Myrtle	T20	Gum, Cider
T7	Beefwood	P40	Crete Dittany	T18	Gum, Red
P13	Bellflower, Dalmation	GC28	Currant, Evergreen	T19	Gum, Red Flowered
GC7	Bergenia, Winterblooming	TS70	Currant, Flowering	T23	Gum, Silver Dollar
GC18	Bishop's Hat	P12	Cushion Bush	T11	Hackberry, Chinese
V22	Black-Eyed Susan	B5	Cyclamen, Miniature	T10	Hackberry, European
P25	Blanket Flower	T15	Cypress, Smooth Arizona	TS66	Hawthorn, India
SS17	Bluebell, Australian	B7	Daffodil	T14	Hawthorn, Washington
TS9	Bottlebrush, Lemon	P6	Daisy, African	TS67	Hawthorn, Yeddo
V1	Bougainvillea	P44	Daisy, Gloriosa	TS49	Heavenly Bamboo
TS47	Box, African	TS28	Daisy, Golden Shrub	TS2	Hibiscus, Blue
T64	Box, Brisbane	P21	Daisy, Mexican	TS37	Holly, Burford Chinese
T47	Box, Victorian	P28	Daylily	SS11	Holly, Dwarf Chinese
SS1	Boxwood, Japanese	P13	Dusty Miller	TS36	Holly, English
SS6	Broom, Kew	P55	Dusty Miller	TS45	Holly Grape, California
TS22	Broom, Moonlight	TS23	Elaeagnus, Thorny	SS13	Holly Grape, Compact
TS74	Brush Cherry, Australian	SS9	Escallonia, Dwarf	TS44	Holly Grape, Oregon
T2	Buckeye, California	TS26	Escallonia, Frade's	AB1	Hollyhock
SS7	Buckwheat, Saffron	TS27	Euonymus, Evergreen	V12	Honeysuckle, Burmese
TS24	Buckwheat, Santa Cruz Island	GC30	Fan Flower	TS75	Honeysuckle, Cape
SS8	Buckwheat, Sulfur	F4	Fern, Autumn	V13	Honeysuckle, Trumpet
TS8	Butterfly Bush	F2	Fern, Holly	T5	Hornbeam, European
T36	Cajeput Tree	F5	Fern, Southern Sword	GC21	Ice Plant
AB2	Calendula	F1	Fern, Sprenger Asparagus	GC22	Ice Plant
TS13	California Lilac, Blue Blossom	F3	Fern, Squirrel's Foot	P31	Iris, Bearded
TS11	California Lilac, Concha	F6	Fern, Western Sword	P29	Iris, Douglas
TS12	California Lilac, Frosty Blue	OG1	Fescue, California	P30	Iris, Scarlet Seeded
GC11	California Lilac, Snowball	P17	Feverfew	T21	Ironbark, Pink Flowered White
TS14	California Lilac, Snow Flurry	T30	Flame Tree, Chinese	V16	Ivy, Boston
B11	Calla Lilly	TS31	Flannel Bush	V3	Ivy, Kangaroo
T12	Carob Tree	TS54	Flax, New Zealand	V11	Jasmine, Pink
P8	Cast Iron Plant	P38	Forget-Me-Not	T40	Jerusalem Thorn
P39	Catmint	TS30	Forsythia	B8	Jessamine, Carolina
V14	Cat's Claw	P37	Four O'Clock	TS38	Juniper, Hollywood
GC9	Ceanothus, Hearst	B6	Freesia, Tecolote Hybrids	TS39	Juniper, Mint Julep
GC8	Ceanothus, Mount Vision	SS3	Fuchsia, Australian	GC23	Juniper, Prostrata
T8	Cedar, Atlas	SS4	Fuchsia, Australian	GC24	Juniper, Silver Spreader
T9	Cedar, Deodar	P60	Fuchsia, California	P15	Jupiter's Beard
GC14	Chamomile	P35	Gay Feather	GC27	Knotweed
TS62	Cherry, Carolina Laurel	GC19	Gazania	V19	Lace Vine, Silver

17

GC31	Lambs Ears	T45	Pine, Japanese Black	P18	Tickseed
P33	Lantana, Trailing	SS15	Pine, Mugo	AB17	Torch Flower
T33	Laurel, Hybrid	T44	Pine, Scots	TS35	Toyon
TS64	Laurel, Portual	TS60	Pine, Yew	V2	Trumpet Creeper
P49	Lavender Cotton, Gray	T46	Pistache, Chinese	V6	Trumpet Vine, Blood Red
P50	Lavender Cotton, Green	T48	Plane Tree, London	V5	Trumpet Vine, Lavendar
P34	Lavender, English	T51	Plum, Purple-leaf	B9	Tulip, Lady
TS69	Lemonade Berry	TS59	Plumbago, Cape	P59	Verbena Hybrid
TS73	Lilac, Common	GC13	Plumbago, Dwarf	TS77	Viburnum, Laurestinus
P4	Lily of the Nile	TS65	Pomegranate	TS76	Viburnum, Sandankwa
P20	Lily, Fortnight	SS16	Pomegranate, Dwarf	GC36	Violet, Sweet
B1	Lily, Peruvian	AB10	Poppy, California	P23	Wallflower
TS40	Lion's Tail	P43	Poppy, Matilija	P22	Wallflower, Siberian
GC26	Lippia	AB12	Poppy, Mexican Tulip	T29	Walnut, Eastern Black
T58	Locust, Idaho	V21	Potato Vine	B10	Watsonia
T16	Loquat, Bronze	GC25	Primrose, Mexican Evening	SS18	Westringia, Rosemary Bush
T17	Loquat, Japanese	TS43	Privet, Japanese,California	T27	Willow, Australian
AB14	Love-in-a-Mist	TS16	Quince, Flowering	V7	Winter Creeper, Common
T28	Maidenhair Tree	P32	Red Hot Poker	V16	Wire Vine, Creeping
TS4	Manzanita, Edmunds	T13	Redbud, Eastern	V24	Wisteria
TS5	Manzanita, McMinn	TS15	Redbud, Western	TS78	Xylosma, Shiny
GC4	Manzanita, Monterey	T62	Redwood, Coast	P3	Yarrow, Common
GC5	Manzanita, Point Reyes	TS18	Rockrose, Crimson Spot	P2	Yarrow, Fernleaf
P16	Marguerite	SS2	Rockrose, Hybrid	GC2	Yarrow, Woolly
P56	Marigold, Bush	TS19	Rockrose, Orchid Spot	SS12	Yaupon, Dwarf
AB9	Marigold, Cape	GC15	Rockrose, Sageleaf	B12	Zephyr Flower
V15	Mattress Vine	TS17	Rockrose, White		
T37	Melaleuca, Prickly	V20	Rose, Cecile Brunner		
TS61	Mint Bush, Roundleafed	V19	Rose, Lady Banks		
TS52	Mock Orange	AB15	Rose, Moss		
P19	Monkey Flower	GC29	Rosemary		
B4	Montbretia	P45	Rue		
TS48	Myrtle, Common	P47	Sage, Autumn		
TS46	Myrtle, Pacific Wax	P46	Sage, Cleveland		
T65	Myrtle, Swamp	TS53	Sage, Jerusalem		
B2	Naked Lady	P48	Sage, Mexican		
AB18	Nasturtium	TS72	Sarcococca, Fragrant		
T53	Oak, Coast Live	B8	Scilla, Peruvian		
T56	Oak, Cork	P36	Sea Lavendar		
T54	Oak, Holly	GC3	Sea Thrift		
T55	Oak, Valley	P52	Sedum, Goldenmoss		
TS50	Oleander	T6	She-Oak, River		
T39	Olive, European	TS32	Silktassel, Coast		
TS51	Olive, Sweet	V18	Silver Lace Vine		
T35	Paperbark, Flaxleaf	TS20	Smokebush		
V17	Passion Vine	GC12	Snow-in-Summer		
T52	Pear, Flowering	P58	Society Garlic		
T61	Pepper Tree, Brazilian	AB5	Spider Flower		
T60	Pepper Tree, California	P24	Spurge		
T3	Peppermint Tree	TS25	St. Catherine's Lace		
TS56	Photinia, Chinese	GC20	St. John's Wort		
TS55	Photinia, Fraser	TS3	Strawberry Tree		
P51	Pincushion Flower	T57	Sumac, African		
AB16	Pincushion Flower	AB11	Sunflower		
T49	Pine, African Fern	T59	Tallow Tree, Chinese		
T41	Pine, Canary Island	TS41	Tea Tree, Australian		
T42	Pine, Eldarica	TS42	Tea Tree, New Zealand		
T43	Pine, Italian Stone	GC33	Thyme		

Plant Index—
Botanic Names

V11	Jasminum polyanthum	
T29	Juglans nigra	
TS38	Juniperus chinensis 'Kaizuka'	
TS39	Juniperus chinensis 'Mint Julep'	
GC23	Juniperus chinensis 'Parsonii'	
GC24	Juniperus virginiana 'Silver Spreader'	
P32	Kniphofia uvaria	
T30	Koelreuteria bipinnata	
T31	Koelreuteria paniculata	
T32	Lagerstroemia indica	
P33	Lantana montevidensis	
T33	Laurus 'Saratoga'	
P34	Lavandula angustifolia, L. dentata	
TS40	Leonotis leonurus	
TS41	Leptospermum laevigatum	
TS42	Leptospermum scoparium cultivars	
P35	Liatris spicata	
TS43	Ligustrum japonicum, L. ovalifolium	
P36	Limonium perezii	
AB13	Lobularia maritima	
V12	Lonicera hildebrandiana	
V13	Lonicera sempervirens	
V14	Macfadyena unguis-cati	
TS44	Mahonia aquifolium	
SS13	Mahonia aquifolium 'Compacta'	
TS45	Mahonia pinnata	
T34	Malus 'Robinson'	
T35	Melaleuca linariifolia	
T36	Meleleuca quinquenervia	
T37	Melaleuca styphelioides	
T38	Metrosideros excelsus	
P37	Mirabilis jalapa	
OG3	Miscanthus sinensis zebrinus	
V15	Muehlenbeckia complexa	
OG4	Muehlenbergia rigens	
P38	Myosotis sylvatica	
TS46	Myrica californica	
TS47	Myrsine africana	
TS48	Myrtus communis	
TS49	Nandina domestica	
SS14	Nandina domestica cultivars	
B7	Narcissus	
P39	Nepeta faassenii	
F5	Nephrolepis cordifolia	
TS50	Nerium oleander	
AB14	Nigella damascena	
GC25	Oenothera berlandierii	
T39	Olea europa	
P40	Origanum dictamnus	
TS51	Osmanthus fragrans	
T40	Parkinsonia aculeata	
V16	Parthenocissus tricuspidata	
V17	Passiflora caerulea	
P41	Pelargonium hortorum	

OG5	Pennisetum alopecuroides	
P42	Penstemon heterophyllus purdyi	
TS52	Philadelphus virginalis	
TS53	Phlomas fruticosa	
TS54	Phormium tenax	
TS55	Photinia fraseri	
TS56	Photinia serrulata	
GC26	Phyla nodiflora	
TS57	Phyllostachys aurea	
T41	Pinus canariensis	
T42	Pinus eldarica	
SS15	Pinus mugo	
T43	Pinus pinea	
T44	Pinus sylvestris	
T45	Pinus thunbergiana	
T46	Pistacia chinensis	
TS58	Pittosporum eugenioides, P. tenuifolium	
T47	Pittosporum undulatum	
T48	Platanus acerifolia	
TS59	Plumbago auriculata	
T49	Podocarpus gracilior	
TS60	Podocarpus macrophylla	
V18	Polygonum aubertii	
GC27	Polygonum capitatum	
F6	Polystichum munitum	
T50	Populus fremontii 'Nevada'	
AB15	Portulaca grandiflora	
TS61	Prostanthera rotundifolia	
TS62	Prunus caroliniana	
T51	Prunus cerasifera cultivars	
TS63	Prunus illicifolia, P. lyonii	
TS64	Prunus lusitanica	
SS16	Punica granatum 'Nana'	
TS65	Punica granatum 'Wonderful'	
T52	Pyrus calleryana cultivars	
T53	Quercus agrifolia	
T54	Quercus ilex	
T55	Quercus lobata	
T56	Quercus suber	
TS66	Rhamnus californica	
TS67	Rhaphiolepis indica	
TS68	Rhaphiolepis umbellata	
TS69	Rhus integrifolia	
T57	Rhus lancea	
TS70	Ribes sanguineum	
TS71	Ribes speciosum	
GC28	Ribes viburnifolium	
T58	Robinia ambigua 'Idahoensis'	
P43	Romneya coulteri	
V19	Rosa banksiae	
V20	Rosa 'Cecile Brunner'	
GC29	Rosmarinum officinalis cultivars	
P44	Rudbeckia hirta	
P45	Ruta graveolens	
P46	Salvia clevelandii	
P47	Salvia greggii	
P48	Salvia leucantha	

P49	Santolina chamaecyparissus	
P50	Santolina virens	
T59	Sapium sebiferum	
TS72	Sarcococca ruscifolia	
P51	Scabiosa columbaria anthemifolia	
AB16	Scabiosa atropurpurea	
GC30	Scaevola 'Mauve Clusters'	
T60	Schinus molle	
T61	Schinus terebinthifolius	
B8	Scilla peruviana	
P52	Sedum acre	
P53	Sedum sieboldii	
P54	Sedum spathulifolium	
P55	Senecio cineraria	
T62	Sequoia sempervirens	
V21	Solanum jasminoides	
SS17	Sollya heterophylla	
T63	Sophora japonica	
GC31	Stachys byzantina	
OG6	Stipa pulchra	
TS73	Syringa vulgaris	
TS74	Syzygium paniculatum	
P56	Tagetes lemonii	
TS75	Tecomaria capensis	
GC32	Teucrium chamaedrys	
P57	Teucrium fruticans	
V22	Thunbergia alata	
GC33	Thymus sp.	
AB17	Tithonia speciosa	
T64	Tristania conferta	
T65	Tristania laurina	
AB18	Tropaeolum majus	
P58	Tulbaghia violacea	
B9	Tulipa clusiana	
P59	Verbena species	
GC34	Verbena tenuisecta	
TS76	Viburnum suspensum	
TS77	Viburnum tinus	
GC35	Viola labradorica	
GC36	Viola odorata	
V23	Vitus vinifera	
B10	Watsonia beatricis, pyramidata	
SS18	Westringia rosmariniformis	
V24	Wisteria species	
TS78	Xylosma congestum	
B11	Zantedeschia aethiopica	
P60	Zauschneria californica	
B12	Zephranthes candida	
T66	Ziziphus jujuba	

Trees

		Important Characteristics				Cultural Preferences					Tolerances						Sunset Zones	Aesthetic and Cultural Compatibility
Plant name and description	Deciduous	Evergreen	Flowers	Fall Color	Fruit	Growth Rate	Full Sun	Part Shade	Well Drained Soil	Monthly Irrigation	No Water After 2nd Yr.	Alkaline Soil	Seacoast Conditions	Sprinklers	Wind	Heat		
T1 — *Acacia baileyana*—Bailey's Acacia Fast growth forming a full head 20 to 30 feet tall and as wide. Silver-gray, finely-divided foliage, and silver-blue, smooth bark and muscular trunk. One to two foot clusters of fragrant yellow flowers hide the foliage in February. Thin canopy in October to avoid broken branches when rain soaks flowers in February. *Acacia baileyana purpurea* produces purple new foliage.		●	●			F	●				●	●		●	●	●	7-9 13-24	T3,8,9 TS7,34,47 SS6,18 V8,9,10 OG3 GC1,10,25 P2,4,9,26 AB9 B7,8
T2 / CN — *Aesculus californica*—California Buckeye Fast with regular watering to 10', slower to 25' to 30' at maturity. Schefflera-like leaves have five 3" to 6" long leaflets. A candelabrum of 8" flower spikes in April. Leaves drop in July in a dry site, will hold on until fall with water. Non-edible 4" fruit.	●		●	●		S-M	●	●			●			●	●	●	14-19	T29,55 TS11,12,14,15 V6,23 GC31
T3 — *Agonis flexuosa*—Peppermint Tree Arching branches and weeping twigs form a graceful 20-foot tall crown 20 to 30 feet wide. Dark green, 3" long pendulous leaves add to the willow-like form. Attractive vertically fissured dark bark and occasional white flower clusters add character. Tolerant of a range of soil conditions. Easily pruned. Marginal in zone 15. Best in 16, 17.		●				F	●	●		●		●	●	●	●		15-17 20-24	T1,42 TS3,9,10,28,40,42 SS13,17 GC4,13 P18,19,28 AB2,7,13,18 V4,6,22 OG1,5 B1
T4 — *Alnus cordata*—Italian Alder Fast growth to 20', then moderate to 40'. Its pyramidal shape is covered with 4" dark green, glossy heart-shaped leaves in summer and creates a beautiful winter silhouette. Some consider the 1" seed "cones" objectionable.		●				M	●	●		●		●		●	●	●	14-24	T14,24 TS6,7,44 GC19,34
T5 — *Carpinus betulus fastigiata*—Upright European Hornbeam A densely twiggy, upright-branching oval form to 40 feet tall. Slow when young. 3" long dark green leaves are deeply veined. No pruning necessary or may be pruned as a hedge. Fall color yellow or tan. Carefree. Does not tolerate wet or alkaline soils. Best in zones 14,15. Tolerates s16.		●				M	●		●			●		●	●	●	3-9 14-17	T23,58 TS1,15,30 SS1,5,16 GC13,17 P1,18,20 AB9,13 V3,7 B4
T6 — *Casuarina cunninghamiana*—River She-Oak To 70' resembling pine or redwood in shape and appearance. Dark green, fine-textured branches. Not misshapen by wind. Tolerant of heat, wind and alkaline/saline soils.		●				F	●					●	●	●	●	●	8-9 13-24	T7 TS23 GC1,6 P36

T1
Bailey's
Acacia

T2
California
Buckeye

T3
Peppermint
Tree

T4
Italian
Alder

T5
Upright
European
Hornbeam

T6
River She-
Oak

22

Trees

	Important Characteristics					Cultural Preferences				Tolerances							Sunset Zones	Aesthetic and Cultural Compatibility
Plant name and description	Deciduous	Evergreen	Flowers	Fall Color	Fruit	Growth Rate	Full Sun	Part Shade	Well Drained Soil	Monthly Irrigation	No Water After 2nd Yr.	Alkaline Soil	Seacoast Conditions	Sprinklers	Wind	Heat		
T7 *Casuarina stricta*—Beefwood To 20' tall forming a broad crown with weeping branches. Texture is coarser than other species. Woody, conelike fruit. Tolerant of dry or wet soil, heat, wind and alkalinity.		●				M	●					●	●	●	●	●	8-9 13-24	T6 TS23 GC1,6 P36
T8 *Cedrus atlantica*—Atlas Cedar Slow to moderate growth reaching 40' to 60' with a stiff, symmetrical appearance. Branch tips point upward. Dark green needles borne in clusters. Needs occasional deep watering. Retains straight terminal leader. *Cedrus atlantica glauca* has silver-blue foliage.		●				M	●					●	●	●	●	●	4-23	T9,41,62 TS41,48 V14 P42,48 B2,7
T9 *Cedrus deodora*—Deodar Cedar Fast growing to 80' tall. Graceful, sweeping branches covered with blue-green needles in clusters. Cones are 4" tall, 3" round standing on top of branches. Recognized by its drooping terminal leader. Too big for many yards.		●				M-F	●				●		●	●	●		4-12 14-24	T8 TS44,72, SS14,17 GC23 P20
T10 *Celtis australis*—European Hackberry Reaches 45' to 75' with a 35' to 50' spread. Gray-green, Elm-like leaves and growth habit. Tolerates heat, wind, drought. Needs deep watering to establish. Resistant to Dutch Elm Disease. Not destructive of pavement.	●					F	●			●		●	●	●	●		8-16 18-20	T24,25 TS3,23,68 P2,11
T11 *Celtis sinensis*—Chinese Hackberry Reaches 30' to 50' tall and broad with upright branching habit. Glossy, dark green, Elm-like leaves. Tolerates wind. Very fast in deep soil with deep watering. Resistant to Dutch Elm Disease. Not tolerant of alkaline, wet soils.	●					F	●					●	●	●			8-16 18-20	T24,25 TS33,65 GC23,32 V14 GC23,32 P59
T12 *Ceratonia siliqua*—Carob Tree Dense, rounded tree, 30' to 40' tall with equal spread. Dark green, compound leaves 8" to 12" long. Females bear numerous 8" pods. Flowers of male plants have strong odor. Budded male plants unavailable. Oak root fungus resistant. Thin crown to prevent winter breakage.		●		●	●	M			●			●	●	●			9 13-16 18-24	T30,31 TS21,23 GC16 P37

T7
Beefwood

CARPOOL IS
2 OR MORE
PERSONS
PER VEHICLE

T8
Blue Atlas
Cedar

T9
Deodar
Cedar

T10
European
Hackberry

T11
Chinese
Hackberry

T12
Carob
Tree

Trees

Plant name and description	Deciduous	Evergreen	Flowers	Fall Color	Fruit	Growth Rate	Full Sun	Part Shade	Well Drained Soil	Monthly Irrigation	No Water After 2nd Yr.	Alkaline Soil	Seacoast Conditions	Sprinklers	Wind	Heat	Sunset Zones	Aesthetic and Cultural Compatibility
T13 *Cercis canadensis*—Eastern Redbud	●		●			S-M	●			●		●				●	1-3 7-20	T51,53 TS11,12,14,16,21 SS14 GC24 P28
T14 *Crataegus phaenopyrum*—Washington Hawthorn	●		●	●	●	M	●			●		●				●	1-11 14-17	T25,26,42,53 TS3,44 SS1,5,9
T15 *Cupressus glabra*—Smooth Arizona Cypress		●				F	●				●	●			●	●	5 8-24	T9 TS23,50 V19 GC6 P25 AB10
T16 *Eriobotrya deflexa*—Bronze Loquat		●	●			F	●	●	●	●						●	8-24	T30,53 TS26 SS9 GC16,17 P2
T17 *Eriobotrya japonica*—Japanese Loquat		●	●	●		M	●	●	●	●						●	4-24	T30,39,43 TS21,23,29 SS1,14 GC19 P22
T18 *Eucalyptus camaldulensis*—Red Gum		●				VF	●				●	●		●	●	●	8-24	T64 TS9,22 GC1,6,20

T13 To 30' tall and as wide in good soil. May be trained in a single-stem or multistem form. Before leaves in March, 3/4" cerise or pink flowers appear on the dark gray stems. The heart-shaped leaves are 3" to 4" broad and dark green. Fall color rosy to rust. Not tolerant of constantly wet clay soil.

T14 A round headed tree to 20' tall, 20' spread. Glossy dark green 2" to 3" leaves are maplelike in shape. Orange and red fall color; 1/2" white flowers in 3" clusters dot the crown in March, followed by clusters of 1/2" orange berries in fall-winter.

T15 To 30'-60' tall. Conical in youth but variable in shape and color. Often becomes open and straggly with age. Silver-gray to dull green foliage. Very drought tolerant when established. Resistant to Cypress canker.

T16 A horizontally branched, umbrella-shaped tree to 18' tall with a 25' spread. The 8" bronze new foliage becomes dark green toothed mature foliage. The clusters of white flowers appear in spring. Monthly deep watering is needed. Susceptible to Fireblight.

T17 Becomes a 15' to 30' tall, 20' to 30' wide umbrella of dark green, deeply ribbed 8" to 12" leaves. Dull white flowers in 6" clusters appear in fall, followed by large seeded, edible 1" orange fruit. Susceptible to fire blight if under stress.

T18 Usually a graceful 50' tree with weeping branches but can also be 80' to 120' tall. Tan, mottled trunk. Inconspicuous flowers. Tolerates wet or alkaline soils and extreme drought. Most commonly used cordwood species. Reseeds into surrounding landscape.

T13 Eastern Redbud

T14 Washingtonton Hawthorn

T15 Smooth Arizona Cypress

T16 Bronze Loquat

T17 Japanese Loquat

T18 Red Gum

Trees

Plant name and description

		Important Characteristics				Cultural Preferences			Tolerances							Sunset Zones	Aesthetic and Cultural Compatibility
		Evergreen / Deciduous	Flowers	Fruit	Fall Color	Growth Rate	Full Sun	Part Shade	Well Drained Soil	Monthly Irrigation	No Water After 2nd Yr.	Alkaline Soil	Seacoast Conditions	Sprinklers	Wind	Heat		
T19	***Eucalyptus ficifolia*—Red Flowered Gum** A round-headed dense crown, to 40' at maturity, usually smaller; 4" dark green, hard, glossy leaves are ornamental. Off-white, orange or red flower clusters cover the crown of the tree in summer. Frost sensitive at 24°F.		•	•		M	•		•	•					•	•	16-17 23-24	T27,35 TS24,25 V10,18 P21 AB2
T20	***Eucalyptus gunnii*—Cider Gum** Narrow, upright growth to 40' to 75' tall with dense, silver-gray foliage. Smooth green and tan bark. White flowers April-June. Tolerant of 10°F. Juvenile foliage similar to that sold in florist shops.		•			F	•	•		•				•	•	•	8-24	T6,49,62 TS48,50,59 V2 GC5,11,24 P11 AB10
T21	***Eucalyptus leucoxylon rosea*—Pink Flowered White Ironbark** Typically produces a rounded, 25' tall semi-open crown, or to 40' if heavily watered. Bright pink flowers in clusters of three are produced most of the summer. Gray-green 4" leaves contrast well with white trunks. Good near coast and in alkaline soils.		•	•		F	•	•				•	•	•	•	•	14-17	T52 TS28,29,56,67 GC8,19 P6,11
T22	***Eucalyptus microtheca*—Coolibah Tree** A graceful single or multi-stemmed tree with blue-green 4" sickle-shaped leaves. The grey or white bark peels in spring in small patches which make little mess. The small white flowers and seed pods create very little litter. The cleanest of 30' to 40' tall Eucalyptus. Tolerant of wind without breakage.		•	•		F	•				•	•	•	•	•	•	8-24	T31,43 TS7,13,22,41 SS4,10,14 V13,16 OG5 AB9,10 GC23,31,32 B6,10
T23	***Eucalyptus polyanthemos*—Silver Dollar Gum** Fast growing to 30' to 60' tall. 15' to 40' wide. Blue-gray, 2" rounded leaves. Bark is gray and fissured when mature. Clusters of small, white flowers in summer. A billowy shape at maturity. Not tolerant of alkaline soils. Not as brittle as many species.		•			F	•							•	•	•	8-24	T36,46 TS19,20,28 GC9 P3,11
T24	***Fraxinus 'Moraine'*—Moraine Ash** An upright crown, to 40' height and 30' spread. Finer textured than most Ash, with dull green foliage, turning bright yellow in fall. Do not use in shallow or heavy clay soils. Resistant to Ash Anthracnose and Aphids.	•			•	F	•		•	•					•		4-24	T31,46,58 TS56,64 GC16 P55 AB2

T19
Red
Flowered
Gum

T20
Cider Gum

T21
Pink
Flowered
White
Ironbark

T22
Coolibah
Tree

T23
Silver
Dollar Gum

T24
Moraine
Ash

28

Trees

	Important Characteristics						Cultural Preferences					Tolerances						
Plant name and description	Evergreen	Deciduous	Flowers	Fall Color	Fruit	Growth Rate	Full Sun	Part Shade	Well Drained Soil	Monthly Irrigation	No Water After 2nd Yr.	Alkaline Soil	Seacoast Conditions	Sprinklers	Wind	Heat	Sunset Zones	Aesthetic and Cultural Compatibility
T25 *Fraxinus oxycarpa 'Raywood'*—Raywood Ash		●				F	●		●					●	●	●	3-9 14-24	T28,31,46 TS1,3 SS1,5,6 GC32 P4,50
T26 *Fraxinus uhdei*—Evergreen Ash	●					VF	●					●	●	●	●	●	12-24	T46,49,53 TS9,21,26 GC16,17,23 P49,57
T27 *Geijera parviflora*—Australian Willow	●					S-M	●	●						●	●	●	8-9 15-24	T39,50 TS6,7,26,28 ss5 P28 AB10
T28 *Ginkgo biloba cultivars*—Maidenhair Tree		●		●		VS	●		●				●	●	●	●	1-9 14-24	T25,39 TS72 SS5,14 GC13
T29 *Juglans nigra*—Eastern Black Walnut		●		●	●	F	●		●			●		●	●	●	1-9 14-24	TS29 SS3,5,6 P16
T30 *Koelreuteria bipinnata*—Chinese Flame Tree		●	●	●	●	M	●	●	●	●		●	●	●	●	●	8-24	T17,31

T25 *Fraxinus oxycarpa 'Raywood'*—Raywood Ash

A rapid growing, oval upright tree to 40' tall. Dark green, leathery leaves turn claret red in fall. A lush, full crown all summer. Seedless and resistant to all the common Ash problems.

T26 *Fraxinus uhdei*—Evergreen Ash

Very fast growing (6' to 15' per year) to 80' tall, 50' spread; use a budded form like 'Majestic Beauty' or 'Sexton' for dark, glossy green leaflets and predictable habit. These forms damaged at 21°F. Seed grown plants are extremely variable in habit. Should never be used in turf or narrow planters due to very destructive roots. Difficult to prune at maturity.

T27 *Geijera parviflora*—Australian Willow

Reaches 25' to 35' tall and wide. Narrow, 3" to 6" long, olive green leaves give the effect of a Weeping Willow. Use root barriers as street tree. A neat, carefree street tree. Does not tolerate inland valley winters or heavy adobe soil. Thin competing main limbs when young.

T28 *Ginkgo biloba cultivars*—Maidenhair Tree

Slow when young, 30' to 50' tall, 80' in old age. Fan shaped leaves turn yellow in fall. Only male forms should be used. 'Autumn Gold' crown to 40'; 'Saratoga' a dense pyramid to 30'; 'Fairmount' a semi-open, perfect pyramid to 50' and faster. Resistant to Oak Root fungus, but not to shallow clay soils.

T29 *Juglans nigra*—Eastern Black Walnut

To 100', usually 60' with a round crown of dark green foliage. Compound leaves 12" to 18" long. Lush green with water, but still attractive without. Aphids a problem over paved areas. Can inhibit growth of surrounding plants. Very long lived.

T30 *Koelreuteria bipinnata*—Chinese Flame Tree

A 20' to 40' tree with a spreading crown; 2' long leaves, divided into many leaflets, turn yellow before dropping in December. 18" terminal clusters of yellow flowers in September-October. Fruit clusters are rust-colored lanterns.

T25
Raywood
Ash

T26
Evergreen
Ash

T27
Australian
Willow

T28
Maidenhair
Tree

T29
Eastern
Black
Walnut

T30
Chinese
Flame
Tree

30

Trees

Plant name and description	Evergreen/Deciduous	Flowers	Fall Color	Fruit	Growth Rate	Well Drained Soil	Part Shade	Full Sun	No Water After 2nd Yr	Monthly Irrigation	Alkaline Soil	Seacoast Conditions	Sprinklers	Wind	Heat	Sunset Zones	Aesthetic and Cultural Compatibility
T31 *Koelreuteria paniculata*—Goldenrain Tree	●	●			M	●							●	●	●	2-21	T17,26,30 TS18,25,59 GC19,29,31 P28
T32 *Lagerstroemia indica*—Crape Myrtle	●	●		●	F	●		●							●	7-9 14-15	T25,28 TS20,26 SS9,14 GC23,24 P42
T33 *Laurus 'Saratoga'*—Hybrid Laurel	●				M	●	●		●		●	●	●	●	●	5-9 12-24	T4,30 TS5,6,23,27 SS1,5,9,11 V5,16,21 OG3 GC26,28,34 P17,21,27 AB4,16 B1,12
T34 *Malus 'Robinson'*—Robinson Crabapple	●	●	●	●	F	●		●						●	●	1-11 14-21	T39,52,61 TS3,6 SS3,13 V4,9,15,16 OG2 GC14,16 P3,4,31,53 AB3 B1,6
T35 *Melaleuca linariifolia*—Flaxleaf Paperbark	●	●			M	●		●					●	●	●	9 12-23	T53,54,56 TS38,39 SS17 GC19,30,31
T36 *Melaleuca quinquenervia*—Cajeput Tree	●	●			M-F	●	●	●				●	●	●	●	9-13 16-17	T6,7 TS24 GC19,21,22 P4,36

T31 — To 20' to 35' high with 10' to 20' rounded crown. Compound leaves are reddish in spring, dull green in summer. Spring flowers in upright, yellow clusters. Lanternlike, 2" seed pods in fall. Roots deep, not invasive.

T32 — A small tree 6' to 30' tall. Fast growing in hot areas. Smooth, gray-brown bark peels to pink inner bark. Red, purple, or white flowers July to September. Water infrequently but deeply. New hybrids *'Natchez', 'Tuscarora'* and *'Muskogee'* are mildew resistant. Not tolerant of high-sodium water.

T33 — Rounded, 4" long, olive green leaves form a semi-open cover over the rounded crown. To 25 feet and as broad. Fast to 15 feet tall, then slower. Inconspicuous dull yellow flowers; no fruit. A very sturdy street tree, patio tree. Prune to any shape, or use as large hedge. Any climate.

T34 — Bronze-green, 3" long leaves turn red-orange in fall. Deep pink flowers follow crimson buds in spring; 3/8" dark red, glossy fruit appears in late summer. A strong, upright grower to 25 feet tall and wide. Will tolerate heavier soils than most Crabapples. Resistant to Fireblight, Mildew.

T35 — A small tree 15' to 25' high. The umbrellalike crown is covered with fluffy white flowers May to June. Bright green, needlelike foliage. The thick bark is white, shredding. Does not tolerate alkaline heavy adobe soil or excessive herbicide use.

T36 — Main trunk(s) upright to 30' with age. Twigs drooping; 3" long leaves are silvery when young, maturing medium green. Bark is thick and spongy, tan peeling to white. White flowers in late summer. Grown as a single trunk or multistem. Excellent next to ocean.

T31
Goldenrain Tree

T32
Crape Myrtle

T33
Hybrid Laurel

T34
Robinson Crabapple

T35
Flaxleaf Paperbark

T36
Cajeput Tree

Trees

Plant name and description	Deciduous	Evergreen	Flowers	Fall Color	Fruit	Growth Rate	Full Sun	Part Shade	Well Drained Soil	Monthly Irrigation	No Water After 2nd Yr	Alkaline Soil	Seacoast Conditions	Sprinklers	Wind	Heat	Sunset Zones	Aesthetic and Cultural Compatibility
T37 *Melaleuca styphelioides*—Prickly Melaleuca		•	•			M-F	•	•					•	•	•	•	9 13-24	T25,49 TS45,47 GC1 P20
T38 *Metrosideros excelsus*—New Zealand Christmas Tree		•	•			M-F	•	•	•				•	•	•	•	16-17	T6,7,19 TS1,5 GC3,4,30 P26,33 AB10
T39 *Olea europea*—European Olive		•		•		M	•		•				•	•	•	•	8-9 11-24	T18 TS11,12,14,22 GC any P16,26
T40 *Parkinsonia aculeata*—Jerusalem Thorn	•		•			F	•		•		•				•	•	11-24	T40,49,62 TS10,16,65,73 SS12,13,14 V10,23 OG6 GC7,30 P16,18,28 AB2,13,18 B5,7,11
T41 *Pinus canariensis*—Canary Island Pine		•				M-F	•							•	•	•	16-18 21-23	T6,8,62 TS9,41,60 GC17,21,22
T42 *Pinus eldarica*—Eldarica Pine		•				F	•			•		•		•	•	•	9-12 15-20	T6,43 TS50,54 SS2 GC8,9,15,20

T37 *Melaleuca styphelioides*—Prickly Melaleuca

To 20' to 40' high. Pendulous branchlets are thickly covered with 1/2" medium green leaves. The thick bark is papery, light tan. White flowers in small "bottlebrushes" appear summer through fall. Excellent lawn tree, even in heavy soil. Oak root fungus resistant.

T38 *Metrosideros excelsus*—New Zealand Christmas Tree

To 30' at maturity, a round headed, dark green glossy ball of 2" leaves when young. Leaves turn gray-green on top, and with woolly white hair beneath as they mature. Flower clusters cover the ends of branches with dark red in May-July. Will grow on the beach.

T39 *Olea europea*—European Olive

A round headed, single or multi-stemmed tree up to 30'. Narrow, gray-green leaves densely cover a healthy specimen. Small white flowers and 3/4" purple fruits are a serious mess over walks. Spray to control fruit. Reseeds into surrounding landscape. Produces quantities of water sprouts if overthinned.

T40 *Parkinsonia aculeata*—Jerusalem Thorn

Fast when young, to 10' x 10' then moderate growth to form a picturesque crown of 20' x 20'. Sparse, 1" light green leaflets thickly cover the pale green, spiny twigs and branches. Yellow, pea-like flowers in quantity in spring and sporadically through the year. Tolerant of dry, alkaline soil. Attractive to gophers.

T41 *Pinus canariensis*—Canary Island Pine

Fast growing to 60' to 80' with pyramidal habit. Hanging, blue-green, 6" needles fully cover the majestic shape. Aphids can be a pest. Tolerates most soils. Oak root fungus resistant. Roots not destructive of pavement.

T42 *Pinus eldarica*—Eldarica Pine

Tall, pyramidal and fast-growing, to 40' tall in 15 years. Dark green when young, slightly grayer-green with age. Excellent Monterey Pine substitute. Tolerant of most soils

T37
Prickly
Melaleuca

T38
New
Zealand
Christmas
Tree

T39
European
Olive

T40
Jerusalem
Thorn

T41
Canary
Island Pine

T42
Eldarica
Pine

34

Trees

Plant name and description	Deciduous	Evergreen	Flowers	Fall Color	Fruit	Growth Rate	Full Sun	Part Shade	Well Drained Soil	Monthly Irrigation	No Water After 2nd Yr.	Alkaline Soil	Seacoast Conditions	Sprinklers	Wind	Heat	Sunset Zones	Aesthetic and Cultural Compatibility
T43 *Pinus pinea*—Italian Stone Pine		•				M	•							•	•	•	•	9-18 21-23	T30,62 TS9,11,12, 14,15,59 GC any P4,20,28
T44 *Pinus sylvestris*—Scot's Pine		•				S	•	•		•		•	•	•	•	•	•	ALL	T50 TS67,73 SS4,16 V9 GC30
T45 *Pinus thunbergiana*—Japanese Black Pine		•				M	•	•	•	•			•	•	•			9-18 21-23	T56,65 TS1,21 SS3,8 GC3,8 P4,6,11
T46 *Pistacia chinensis*—Chinese Pistache	•			•		M	•		•		•			•		•		8-16 18-23	TS16,21,40 GC8,13,16 P20,28
T47 *Pittosporum undulatum*—Victorian Box		•	•	•	•	M	•	•	•	•					•			16-17 21-24	T40,49,62 TS10,16,65, 78 SS12,13,14 V10,23 OG6 GC7,30 P16,18,28 AB2,13,18 B5,7,11
T48 *Platanus acerifolia*—London Plane Tree	•			•		F	•	•	•		•			•		•		2-24	T28,62 TS1,3 GC3,4,9 P3,4,11,20

T43 *Pinus pinea*—Italian Stone Pine

A massive, dark green ball when young. To 40' to 80' tall at maturity with a flat umbrellalike crown. Long, dark green needles. Moderate growth rate. Excellent at the beach or desert. Too large for most gardens. Large limbs equal to trunk diameter can fall out of the tree if not thinned.

T44 *Pinus sylvestris*—Scot's Pine

Moderate growth to 70'+ with age. Short, stiff blue-green needles create a semiopen canopy. Branching becomes irregular and picturesque with age, mindful of *Pinus thunbergiana*. Reddish young bark and checkered older bark are attractive. Small reddish cones.

T45 *Pinus thunbergiana*—Japanese Black Pine

Depending on soil and nutrients, 20' to 30'. The favorite Japanese garden pine. An asymmetrical, often leaning habit. Stiff, dark green needles, producing clusters of foliage. Easily pruned to any shape. Susceptible to Bark Aphids.

T46 *Pistacia chinensis*—Chinese Pistache

To 30' to 40' tall with a round crown. Dark green, 8" compound leaves. Brilliant orange and red fall colors. Grows best in hot climates with deep soil but tolerates most soils. Pest free. Non-destructive root system. Resistant to oak root fungus.

T47 *Pittosporum undulatum*—Victorian Box

Moderate growth to 15' x 15', then slower to 30' x 30'. Dark green 2-1/2 inch long wavy-margined leaves densely cover the round crown. The gray bark, beautiful branching and intensely fragrant white flowers in spring add character. Side branches should be removed from trunk gradually over three years. Some Aphids in spring and Brown Scale are occasional problems.

T48 *Platanus acerifolia*—London Plane Tree

A dependable performer if Anthracnose, Mildew and Scale are controlled. The 8" wide maple-like leaves have white woolly undersides causing allergies for some people. Left unpruned, they will be 50' tall, pyramids. *'Bloodgood'* not resistant to mildew. *'Yarwood'* resistant to mildew and Anthracnose. *'Centennial'* reported to be mildew resistant.

T43
Italian
Stone Pine

T44
Scot's
Pine

T45
Japanese
Black Pine

T46
Chinese
Pistache

T47
Victorian
Box

T48
London
Plane
Tree

36

Trees

Plant name and description	Important Characteristics						Cultural Preferences			Tolerances							Sunset Zones	Aesthetic and Cultural Compatibility
	Evergreen/Deciduous	Flowers	Fall Color	Fruit	Growth Rate	Well Drained Soil	Part Shade	Full Sun	Monthly Irrigation	No Water After 2nd Yr.	Alkaline Soil	Seacoast Conditions	Sprinklers	Wind	Heat		
T49 *Podocarpus gracilior*—African Fern Pine	●				M-F	●	●	●	●				●		●	8-9 12-24	T62,64 TS63,65,78 GC17,19,20, 21,22
T50 *Populus fremontii Nevada*—Nevada Male Cottonwood	●		●		VF	●	●		●				●	●	●	7-24	T43,52 TS67,68,72, 74 SS14 GC4,30 P54
T51 *Prunus cerasifera cultivars*—Purpleleaf Plum	●	●	●		M	●		●	●				●		●	2-22	T6,41,42 TS29,45 SS1,5,14 V20 GC6 P4
T52 *Pyrus calleryana cultivars*—Flowering Pear	●	●	●		● M	●			●			●		●	●	2-9 14-21	T51,53,58 TS1,47 GC3,4,17 P1,4,6,11 AB3
T53 CN *Quercus agrifolia*—Coast Live Oak	●				M	●	●	●					●	●	●	7-10 12 14-24	T51,52,55 TS1,66,68, 70,71 SS14 GC3,4,16,28 P19,29,38, 42
T54 *Quercus ilex*—Holly Oak	●				M	●		●		●	●	●	●	●	●	4-24	T56,58 TS7,11 SS5 GC1 P4,20,25

T49 *Podocarpus gracilior*—African Fern Pine

Fine-textured, pendulous growth if produced from cuttings. To 40' tall and as broad if produced from seed. Soft, gray-green leaves create a billowing growth on a strong upright trunk. Good as a patio tree if root barriers used. Not for alkaline or wet clay soils. Damaged at 22°F.

T50 *Populus fremontii Nevada*—Nevada Male Cottonwood

A 40' to 60' oval upright form. Brilliant green 4" leaves turn butter yellow in the fall. Every breeze moves the leaves. Very drought tolerant. This male clone doesn't create the messy "cotton" for which they are famous. Very invasive roots.

T51 *Prunus cerasifera cultivars*—Purpleleaf Plum

Most mature at 25' to 30' tall and as wide. 'Thundercloud'—some fruit, flowers light pink, dark foliage; 'Krauter's Vesuvius'—no fruit, flowers light pink, darkest foliage; 'Prunus blireiana'—double pink flowers, few fruit. Aphid problem in spring, bronze foliage. None good in dense soils in lawn.

T52 *Pyrus calleryana cultivars*—Flowering Pear

'Aristocrat' is pyramidal when young becoming oval upright to 40' x 30'. 'Redspire' more pyramidal. 'Bradford' may reach 40' tall, 25' wide and be semideciduous in warmest areas. (Occasionally light infections of Fireblight.) Brilliant red fall color, masses of white flowers in spring. No fruit. Tolerant of alkaline and dense soils.

T53 CN *Quercus agrifolia*—Coast Live Oak

The dark green domes which dominate California coastal hillsides. To 40' tall, 70' spread (or 70' tall, 40' spread in groves). 2" dark shining green, rounded leaves with spined edges. Limbs and branches are twisting, gray. Fast growth when young. Do not use in lawn, or with other water loving understory.

T54 *Quercus ilex*—Holly Oak

A dense, oval upright crown 40' to 70' tall with equal spread. Dull green 2" to 3" leaves with silver undersides. This species is so variable from seed that no two will look alike. May be sheared as a hedge. Reseeds into landscape. Tolerant of alkaline soil and seaside sites, but not dense clay in lawn.

T49
African
Fern Pine

T50
Nevada
Male
Cotton-
wood

T51
Purple-leaf
Plum

T52
Flowering
Pear

T53
Coast Live
Oak

T54
Holly Oak

38

Trees

Plant name and description	Important Characteristics					Cultural Preferences			Tolerances									Aesthetic and Cultural Compatibility
	Deciduous	Evergreen	Flowers	Fall Color	Fruit	Growth Rate	Full Sun	Part Shade	Well Drained Soil	Monthly Irrigation	No Water After 2nd Yr.	Alkaline Soil	Seacoast Conditions	Sprinklers	Wind	Heat	Sunset Zones	
T55 CN *Quercus lobata*—Valley Oak — Appearing in areas with year round water availability. Magnificent structure, reaches 70' high and broad with picturesque twisted branches. Gray, checkered bark. Medium gray, 2" lobed leaves with pale undersides. Fast growing when young. Good in riparian areas. Treat for Oak Pit Scale in winter. Do not use in lawns.	●					M	●		●		●				●	● ●	1-3 6-16 18-21	T53,61 TS63,66,68, 70,71 GC3,4,6,28 P19,38,42
T56 *Quercus suber*—Cork Oak — Similar in shape to Coast Live Oak, but growing to 30' tall. Foliage olive green on upper side, gray on underside. Spiny, convex 1" to 1-1/2" leaves. Massive trunks, thick corky bark. Very drought tolerant. Drops old foliage in late spring. Over-fertilizing results in heavy Aphid infestation.		●				M	●	●	●	●					●	● ●●	8-16 18-28	T55,61 TS1,3,4,5 GC3,4,6,23 P5,29,38,42
T57 *Rhus lancea*—African Sumac — To 25' with dense, round crown. Fast growing when young. Graceful, weeping outer branches. Leathery, dark green leaves of three leaflets. Small red berries. Suckers are a problem when young. Excellent in desert. Good as single or multistem.		●				F	●			●				●		●	8-9 12-24	T46,56 TS1,48 SS1,14,17 GC6,8,9 P4,5,21,32, 44
T58 *Robinia ambigua 'Idahoensis'*—Idaho Locust — To 40' with upright branching. Medium green leaves to 12" long divided into 13 to 15, 1-1/2" leaflets. Flowers like deep pink Wisteria in drooping, 8" clusters in late spring. Does not reseed. Must prune to form structure first two years.	●		●		●	VF	●		●					●	●	●	ALL	T4,13,14 TS3,17,18, 19,29 GC5,6,8,9, 11,23,24 P20
T59 *Sapium sebiferum*—Chinese Tallow Tree — Round, light green, 2-1/2" heart-shaped leaves flutter in the breeze. They turn a translucent mixture of red, orange, yellow in fall. Maturing at 30 feet with training or as a large shrub. The round crown may be scattered with 5" long pendulous clusters of small yellow flowers in summer, followed by waxy white 1/2" seeds. Oak Root Fungus resistant.	●		●		●	S-M	●		●	● ●				●		●	8-9 12-16 18-21	T4,9,24 TS62,66 SS1,17 GC28
T60 *Schinus molle*—California Pepper Tree — Fast growing to 25' to 40' high, 30' to 60' broad. Gnarled tan trunk, weeping branches; bright green, pinnately compound leaves create a lacy look. Clusters of rose-colored berries in fall. Little care needed. Susceptible to Verticillium Wilt disease, Pepper Tree Psyllid, and Oak Root Fungus.	●		●		●	F	●			● ●		● ●	●	●		●	8-9 12-24	T18,26 TS56,65,78 SS3 GC16,17,20 P28

T55
Valley Oak

T56
Cork Oak

T57
African
Sumac

T58
Idaho Locust

T59
Chinese
Tallow Tree

T60
California
Pepper
Tree

40

Trees

	Plant name and description	Deciduous	Evergreen	Flowers	Fall Color	Fruit	Growth Rate	Full Sun	Part Shade	Well Drained Soil	Monthly Irrigation	No Water After 2nd Yr.	Alkaline Soil	Seacoast Conditions	Sprinklers	Wind	Heat	Sunset Zones	Aesthetic and Cultural Compatibility
T61	***Schinus terebinthifolius*—Brazilian Pepper** To 15' to 30' high often with a flat crown. Glossy, dark green, compound leaves are of medium texture. Bright red berries in winter. Water infrequently and deeply to discourage surface roots.		●	●			M	●								●	● ●	1-3 6-16 18-21	T53,61 TS63,66,68, 70,71 GC3,4,6,28 P19,38,42
T62 CN	***Sequoia sempervirens*—Coast Redwood** Tall, fast and pyramidal to 50', up to 100' at maturity. Cutting grown forms are *'Soquel'* - dense, gray-green, slower growing; *'Aptos Blue'* - semiopen habit, green with gray undersides, fast; *'Los Altos'* - dark glossy green, semiopen, fast; *'Santa Cruz'* - paler green full, moderate. Must receive regular irrigation to remain disease free.		●				F	●	●		●				●	●	●	15-17 19-24	T54,62 TS67,69 GC16,17,20 AB8
T63	***Sophora japonica*—Chinese Scholar Tree** Moderate growth to 15' tall, 20' wide, then slow to 40' tall. Green bark on young branches; the 8" long, dark green compound leaves are divided into 11 to 17 1-1/2" leaflets; 8" to 12" terminal clusters of creme-colored flowers appear in summer, which are messy. Tolerant of most soils. Oak Root Fungus resistant. *'Regent'* is an improved, faster-growing form.	●		●			M	●	●		●					●	●	ALL	T41,49 TS4,5,44, 46,70,72 GC3 P8,21,22,38
T64	***Tristania conferta*—Brisbane Box** An oval-upright habit covered with oval 4" to 6" leathery leaves. Handsome reddish brown, smooth bark peels to reveal light tan new bark. Creamy-white flowers in summer. A good street tree and substitute for Eucalyptus, it can reach 40' with a 30' spread.		●	● ●			F	●		●	●		●		●	● ●	●	19-24 15-18	T46 TS18,22,27 SS1,4,15 V8,11 OG4 GC7,32,35 P10,35,39 AB5 B5
T65	***Tristania laurina*—Swamp Myrtle** A densely foliaged, elegant small tree. Grow as a multi-stem or singlestem specimen. Glossy green 4" long, narrow leaves are background for 1/4" yellow, fragrant flowers. White bark is a pleasant contrast. Easily pruned to any shape. Good container plant.		●	● ●			S-M	●	●		●				●	●	●	19-24 15-18	T48,52 TS59,72,76 SS5 GC4,19 P8,26
T66	***Ziziphus jujuba*—Chinese Date** Glossy, bright green 2" leaves produce a light canopy over the somewhat spiny pendulous branches. Slow growth to 20'. Tolerates alkaline soil and drought but much healthier with some water. 2" fruit which are delicious green or dried are borne in summer. Yellow fall color.	●			● ●		M	●			●		● ●		●	● ●	●	7-16	T25,65 TS8,27,30 SS11,12,13 V2,18 OG3 GC12,13,14 P1,4,9,20 AB13 B6,11

T61
Brazilian
Pepper

T62
Coast
Redwood

T63
Chinese
Scholar
Tree

T64
Brisbane
Box

T65
Swamp
Myrtle

T66
Chinese
Date

Plant name	Deciduous	Evergreen	Flowers	Fall Color	Fruit	Growth Rate	Full Sun	Part Shade	Well Drained Soil	Monthly Irrigation	No Water After 2nd Yr	Alkaline Soil	Seacoast Conditions	Sprinklers	Wind	Heat	Sunset Zones	Aesthetic and Cultural Compatibility
TS1 *Abelia grandiflora*—Glossy Abelia			●	●		F	●	●		●				●	●	●	5-24	T59 TS21,26 SS1,14 GC4 P4,21,25
TS2 *Alyogyne huegelii*—Blue Hibiscus		●	●			F	●		●			●			●		15-17 20-24	T13 TS11,12,14, 17-19 GC6,8,9,13 AB3
TS3 *Arbutus unedo*—Strawberry Tree		●	●		●	S-M	●	●				●	●	●	●		4-24	T2,39,48 TS4,5,74,78 GC4,5 P33
TS4 CN *Artostaphylos bakeri 'Louis Edmunds'*—Edmunds Manzanita		●	●			M	●	●			●				●	●	4-9 14-17	T16,24,25 TS5,7,12,14, 35,45,63 GC4,6 P19,21
TS5 CN *Artostaphylos densiflora 'Howard McMinn'*—McMinn Manzanita		●	●			M	●	●	●					●	●	●	7-9 14-21	T2,12,14 TS3,4,7,15 GC4,6 P3,25 AB10
TS6 *Berberis darwinii*—Darwin's Barberry		●	●		●	S-M	●	●	●						●	●	1-11 14-17	T4,12,53 TS35,60 SS14 GC30 P49

TS1 — *Abelia grandiflora*—Glossy Abelia

Forms an arching mound 3' to 8' tall. Shiny leaves are reddish-bronze in the spring and fall. Flowers are white or tinged pink in June and October. Needs some water. Should be hand pruned, not sheared. *A.g. 'Sherwoodii'* is densely covered with smaller maroon foliage, and reaches 4' tall. *A.g. prostrata* is a groundcover.

TS2 — *Alyogyne huegelii*—Blue Hibiscus

The 3" foliage is like that of some scented geraniums. An upright, semi-open shrub to 6' tall; 4" lilac, glossy, pinwheel flowers from April to June, then a scattering at other times. *'Santa Cruz'* has darker flowers and a more compact habit.

TS3 — *Arbutus unedo*—Strawberry Tree

Usually a rounded shrub to 8', it can become a 25' tree. White bell-like flowers in clusters on branch tips fall and winter, along with strawberrylike fruit. Slow growth without water, moderate with water and annual fertilizing. Good screen. Greenhouse thrips may be a problem in the shade.

TS4 CN — *Artostaphylos bakeri 'Louis Edmunds'*—Edmunds Manzanita

An upright branching habit to 5' tall. The semiopen habit allows a view of the mahogany colored stems through the gray-green 1-1/2" leaves. Medium pink flowers appear earlier in spring than other Manzanitas. Less susceptible to root diseases than most.

TS5 CN — *Artostaphylos densiflora 'Howard McMinn'*—McMinn Manzanita

Forms a 3' to 5' mound with a 7' spread. Glossy, bright green, 1" leaves. Smooth, reddish-black bark. White to pink flowers in 3" clusters cover the plant from February to April. The most dependable of the Manzanitas. Even good sheared.

TS6 — *Berberis darwinii*—Darwin's Barberry

A dense, 5' to 7' mound of dark, glossy 1" leaves. Masses of orange-buff flowers cover branches in summer. Dark blue berries in fall are excellent bird food. Good barrier plant due to spiny foliage. Inside foliage will be killed if sprinklers strike it.

TS1
Glossy
Abelia

TS2
Blue
Hibiscus

TS3
Strawberry
Tree

TS4
Edmunds
Manzanita

TS5
McMinn
Manzanita

TS6
Darwin's
Barberry

44

Tall Shrubs

Plant name and description	Important Characteristics					Cultural Preferences			Tolerances								Aesthetic and Cultural Compatibility
	Evergreen/Deciduous	Flowers	Fall Color	Fruit	Growth Rate	Full Sun	Part Shade	Well Drained Soil	Monthly Irrigation	No Water After 2nd Yr.	Alkaline Soil	Seacoast Conditions	Sprinklers	Wind	Heat	Sunset Zones	
TS7 — *Berberis thunbergii*—Japanese Barberry	●	●		●	M	●			●		●		●	●	●	1-11 14-17	T41,45 TS4,33 SS14 GC30 P49
TS8 — *Buddlera davidii*—Butterfly Bush	●	●			F	●	●		●			●	●		●	1-9 12-24	T41 TS11,23,25 SS17,18 V16,17 OG5 GC10,13 P4,9,11 AB1,7,18 B1,11
TS9 — *Callistemon citrinus*—Lemon Bottlebrush	●	●			F	●			●			●	●	●	●	8-9 12-24	T8,18,56 TS26,41,60 SS5,9 GC16 P1,20,21
TS10 CN — *Carpenteria californica*—Bush Anemone	●	●			S	●	●		●						●	5-9 14-24	T53,55 TS4,32 SS13,14 V8 GC13,18,28 AB10 B5
TS11 CN — *Ceanothus 'Concha'*	●	●			F-M	●	●			●				●	●	4-7 14-24	T2,13 TS17-20,31 SS5 GC6,8,9,11,19 P60
TS12 CN — *Ceanothus 'Frosty Blue'*—Frosty Blue California Lilac	●	●			VF	●				●				●	●	4-7 14-24	T2,13 TS11,14-16 SS5 GC6,8,9,19,23 AB10

TS7 Berberis thunbergii—Japanese Barberry

Spiny leaves on arching branches, 4' to 6' tall with equal spread. Yellow or orange flowers in the fall, then red berries. Dull green 1" leaves, or *'Atropurpurea'* has maroon foliage. Either may be sheared as a hedge. Fall color can be spectacular.

TS8 Buddlera davidii—Butterfly Bush

A 10' to 12' tall, arching shrub. The 6" leaves lightly cover the 4' to 6' long spring shoots. They are tipped by 8" to 12" long dense spikes of small purple to pink flowers in summer. These fragrant flowers are attractive to butterflies. White forms are not as satisfactory. Prune to 12" to 18" tall in winter.

TS9 Callistemon citrinus—Lemon Bottlebrush

To 15' tall and broad if unpruned or may be sheared as a hedge. Bright red tufts of stamens form a bottlebrushlike flower cluster. Severe alkalinity or some herbicides cause chlorosis in the normally dark green 1-1/2" long foliage. Very tough. May cause allergies.

TS10 CN Carpenteria californica—Bush Anemone

This 3' to 4' tall shrub has stiff vertical branches covered with 3" dark glossy green leaves. The 2" wide white flowers are borne in clusters over much of the plant from May through August. Cut oldest canes out at 4" from the ground semi-annually. Use in filtered shade in zones 14, 15.

TS11 CN Ceanothus 'Concha'

This shrub is 5' to 7' tall, 6' to 8' in spread; the small glandular dark green leaves are less palatable to deer than broadleaved forms. Pink buds open to fluorescent blue flowers. The similar 'Dark Star' is much broader than tall. More disease resistant than most Ceanothus.

TS12 CN Ceanothus 'Frosty Blue'—Frosty Blue California Lilac

To 13' tall and broad, this is the fastest of the garden tolerant upright Ceanothus. Round, dark green 3/4" leaves are held on stiff upright branches. Deep blue flowers in dense 3-1/2" clusters in midspring turn to a silvery color, continuing to be attractive.

TS7
Japanese
Barberry

TS8
Butterfly
Bush

TS9
Lemon
Bottlebrush

TS10
Bush
Anemone

TS11
Ceanothus
'Concha'

TS12
Frosty
Blue
California
Lilac

Tall Shrubs

	Important Characteristics					Cultural Preferences				Tolerances							Sunset Zones	Aesthetic and Cultural Compatibility
Plant name and description	Deciduous	Evergreen	Flowers	Fall Color	Fruit	Growth Rate	Well Drained Soil	Part Shade	Full Sun	No Water After 2nd Yr	Monthly Irrigation	Alkaline Soil	Seacoast Conditions	Sprinklers	Wind	Heat		
TS13 CN *Ceanothus thyrsiflorus 'Skylark'*—Skylark Blueblossom A 4' to 6' tall, dense mound of 2" glossy leaves; 2' to 3' clusters of dark blue flowers cover the plant throughout spring. Less susceptible to overwatering than many cultivars.			●	●		F	●		●	●	●		●		●	●	4-7 14-24	T33,52,55 TS12,14,15, 30 SS8,13,15 V14,17,22 OG1,2 P7,12,15 AB4,10,12 B2,7
TS14 CN *Ceanothus thyrsiflorus 'Snow Flurry'* Large clusters of snow-white flowers contrast with the waxed look of bright green foliage in midspring. From 6' to 15' depending on soil quality and moisture. The 2" long leaves fully cover the plant.			●	●		F	●		●		●		●		●	●	4-7 14-24	T2,13 TS11,12,15, 16,31 SS5 GC6,8,9,11, 19 AB10
TS15 CN *Cercis occidentalis*—Western Redbud Usually an 8' to 12' cluster of upright stems. Gray-green, 3" round leaves. Flowers are pink to intense magenta for 3 weeks in spring. Where winters are below 28°F, foliage provides rose fall color. Resistant to Oak Root fungus, but very sensitive to root diseases if over watered. Plant as young as possible.	●		●		●	F	●		●		●		●		●	●	2-24	T2,15 TS11,12,14, 24,25,29,31 SS7,8 GC1,4,6 AB10
TS16 *Chaenomeles cultivars*—Flowering Quince A tangled mass of angular twigs best used as a background. One of the survivors in any old, unwatered garden, they come in all sizes of plant, from 2' tall, 5' broad *'Cameo'* with double salmon flowers to the 6' to 8' tall *'Hollandia'* with large red flowers. Dark green 2" to 4" leaves appear after the spring bloom.	●		●		●	F-M	●	●		●	●			●		●	1-21	T13 TS1,3 SS1,14 V24 GC20,24 P4
TS17 *Cistus hybridus*—White Rockrose A dense, rounded shrub 2' to 5' tall and 3' to 8' broad. Crinkly, gray-green leaves. White, 1-1/2" flowers with yellow centers in late spring. Shears very well. Good on south-facing slopes. Best in well drained soils near the ocean.			●	●		F	●						●	●	●	●	7-9 12-15 18-22 best, 16,17 23,24	T23,46 TS21,50,55, 56 GC1,6,8,9, 11 P3,6,16
TS18 *Cistus ladanifer*—Crimson Spot Rockrose Compact, 3' to 5' rounded shrub. Shiny, dark green 2" leaves are fragrant in heat. White, 3" flowers have a dark red spot at the base of each petal. Blooms all summer. This species resents shearing. Excellent near the coast.			●	●		F	●		●				●	●	●	●	7-9 12-15 18-22 best, 17-23 24	T16,17 TS21,50,55, 56 GC1,6,8,9, 11 P16

TS13
Skylark
Blue-
blossom

TS14
Snow
Flurry

TS15
Western
Redbud

TS16
Flowering
Quince

TS17
White
Rockrose

TS18
Crimson
Spot
Rockrose

Tall Shrubs

	Important Characteristics				Cultural Preferences				Tolerances								Sunset Zones	Aesthetic and Cultural Compatibility
Plant name and description	Deciduous	Evergreen	Flowers	Fall Color	Fruit	Growth Rate	Full Sun	Part Shade	Well Drained Soil	Monthly Irrigation	No Water After 2nd Yr.	Alkaline Soil	Seacoast Conditions	Sprinklers	Wind	Heat		

TS19 *Cistus purpureus*—Orchid Spot Rockrose

To 4' tall, usually less. Spreading mound of dull green 1-1/2" leaves. Bright, reddish-purple 3" flowers have a red spot at the base of each petal and appear June to July. Good in firebreak areas.

Characteristics: Flowers ●, Fall Color ●; Growth Rate F; Full Sun ●, Part Shade ●; Tolerances: Sprinklers ●, Wind ●, Heat ● ●. Sunset Zones: 7-9, 12-15, 18-22 best, 17, 23, 24. Aesthetic: T23,46 TS28,32 GC1,9,31

TS20 *Cotinus coggygria*—Smokebush

Depending on exposure, 8' to 25' tall and as broad. Semiopen, twiggy habit with 3" soft green leaves. Flowers are puffs at the end of branches. 'Royal Purple' has purple foliage and flower puffs. Excellent rust and rose fall color. Must have good drainage.

Characteristics: Deciduous ●, Flowers ●, Fruit ●; Growth Rate F; Full Sun ●, Part Shade ●; Tolerances: Alkaline Soil ●; Heat ●. Sunset Zones: 10,11 14-16. Aesthetic: T8,9,23 TS29,32 P57

TS21 *Cotoneaster lacteus*—Red Clusterberry

A shrub 6' to 8' tall or trained as a small tree to 15'. Leathery 4" gray-green leaves with white hairy undersides. White flowers in 4" to 6" clusters. Long lasting, bright red fruit appears in 4" clusters in fall.

Characteristics: Flowers ●, Fall Color ●, Fruit ●; Growth Rate F; Full Sun ●, Part Shade ●; Well Drained Soil ●; Heat ● ● ●. Sunset Zones: 4-24. Aesthetic: T12,13,17 TS54,59 GC16,17,23 P31,37

TS22 *Cytisus praecox* 'Warminster'—Moonlight Broom

Compact mass of green leafless twigs, 3' to 5' high with 4' to 6' spread. Pale yellow to white flowers March to April. Can be a nuisance if it reseeds into the garden.

Characteristics: Flowers ●, Fall Color ●; Growth Rate F; Full Sun ●; Tolerances: Seacoast Conditions ●; Sprinklers ●, Wind ●, Heat ● ●. Sunset Zones: 2-9, 12-22. Aesthetic: T18 TS16-18, 52-54 GC8,9,11, 19

TS23 *Elaeagnus pungens*—Thorny Elaeagnus

Thorny, impenetrable shrub 8' to 15' tall. Small, fragrant white flowers in late fall, red berries in spring. Selected forms are almost thornless. 'Fruitlandii' has rich green, 5" leaves with silver scales. All easily pruned to any shape. Tolerant of alkaline and wet soil condition.

Characteristics: Flowers ●, Fall Color ●, Fruit ●; Growth Rate F; Full Sun ●, Part Shade ●, Well Drained Soil ●; No Water After 2nd Yr. ●, Alkaline Soil ●; Sprinklers ●, Wind ●, Heat ●. Sunset Zones: 4-24. Aesthetic: T7,8,12,15, 17 TS59,68 SS2 GC1,15 AB10 P25

TS24 CN *Eriogonum arborescens*—Santa Cruz Island Buckwheat

To 3' to 4' tall, spreading 5'. Narrow 1" gray-green leaves are clustered at branchlet ends. Creamy flowers borne in 18" wide flat clusters during summer. Useful in dried flower arrangements.

Characteristics: Flowers ●, Fall Color ●, Fruit ●; Growth Rate F; No Water After 2nd Yr. ●, Alkaline Soil ●; Sprinklers ●; Wind ●, Heat ● ●. Sunset Zones: 14-24. Aesthetic: T19 TS11,12,14, 31 SS7 GC6,8 P43

TS19
Orchid Spot
Rockrose

TS20
Smokebush

TS21
Red
Cluster-
berry

TS22
Moonlight
Broom

TS23
Thorny
Elaeagnus

TS24
Santa
Cruz
Island
Buck-
wheat

Tall Shrubs

Plant name and description	Deciduous	Evergreen	Flowers	Fall Color	Fruit	Growth Rate	Full Sun	Part Shade	Well Drained Soil	Monthly Irrigation	No Water After 2nd Yr	Alkaline Soil	Seacoast Conditions	Sprinklers	Wind	Heat	Sunset Zones	Aesthetic and Cultural Compatibility
TS25 CN *Erigonum giganteum*—St. Catherine's Lace		●	●		●	F	●				●		●		●	●	14–24	T19 TS2,23,24 SS2,7,8 GC11,15 P43
TS26 *Escallonia exoniensis 'Frades'*		●	●			M	●	●		●			●	●	●	●	14–17	T16,53 TS1,23 SS9 GC1,6,8,13 P4
TS27 *Euonymus japonica*—Evergreen Euonymus		●	●			M	●					●	●	●	●	●	2–20	T46 TS4,6,7 SS1,5,11 V2 OG6 GC5,20,32 P50,52 AB11,13 B1
TS28 *Euryops pectinatus*—Golden Shrub Daisy		●	●			F	●				●		●	●	●	●	14–17 19–24	T21,23 TS32 GC8,19 P5,32,33
TS29 *Feijoa sellowiana*—Pineapple Guava		●	●		●	M	●	●						●	●	●	7–9 12–24	T17,21 TS49,58,59 GC16,17,23 P48 AB3
TS30 *Forsythia x intermedia*—Forsythia	●		●			M	●	●				●	●	●	●	●	2–11 14–16 18,19	T4,24 TS12,13,20 SS13,15 V18 OG3 GC31,36 P38,44 AB18 B3,7

TS25 CN — *Erigonum giganteum*—St. Catherine's Lace
Spreading, semi-open, 3' to 8' mound with grayish-white 1-1/2" oval leaves. Pale pink to cream flowers in 2' to 3' broad flat clusters. Long blooming period. Best in well-drained soil and near the ocean, but tolerant of unwatered inland conditions. Useful for dried flower arrangements.

TS26 — *Escallonia exoniensis 'Frades'*
To 6' tall and as wide if unpruned, but usually seen sheared to a geometric form. The dark green 1-1/2" leaves fully cover the plant, acting as a background for the rose-colored tubular flowers. These flowers are scattered over the plant almost all year. Must be watered monthly to avoid disease susceptibility.

TS27 — *Euonymus japonica*—Evergreen Euonymus
An excellent substitute for Texas Privet, this shrub will reach 10' tall with age or may be sheared to any size. Powdery mildew is a problem in shade or with poor air movement. Tolerant of any soil condition. Gold and green and green and white forms are available.

TS28 — *Euryops pectinatus*—Golden Shrub Daisy
A rounded plant to 3' to 6' with gray-green foliage and twigs. Covered with 2" bright yellow daisies in spring and summer. Excellent near the ocean. Prune to 18" in spring and fertilize. New growth will reappear immediately.

TS29 — *Feijoa sellowiana*—Pineapple Guava
A many-stemmed 10' to 25' shrub which can be pruned to almost any shape. Glossy green 2" to 3" leaves hide the delicious 2" to 3" gray-green fruit. The 1" red flowers are also edible. May be trained as a small tree. Beautiful tan bark.

TS30 — *Forsythia x intermedia*—Forsythia
Stiff, arching branches to 10' tall are coated with pale- to butter-yellow flowers in February, before leaves appear. The leaves are 2" long and a medium green which blends well with Oaks. Cut 1/3 of flowering stems to ground in March. *'Lynwood Gold'* is upright to 7' tall, *'Spring Glory'* bears heavy crops of pale yellow flowers.

TS25
St.
Catherine's
Lace

TS26
Frades
Escallonia

TS27
Evergreen
Euonymus

TS28
Golden
Shrub Daisy

TS29
Pineapple
Guava

TS30
Forsythia

52

Tall Shrubs

Plant name and description	Important Characteristics					Cultural Preferences				Tolerances							Sunset Zones	Aesthetic and Cultural Compatibility
	Deciduous	Evergreen	Flowers	Fall Color	Fruit	Growth Rate	Well Drained Soil	Full Sun	Part Shade	Monthly Irrigation	No Water After 2nd Yr.	Alkaline Soil	Seacoast Conditions	Sprinklers	Wind	Heat		
TS31 CN *Fremontodendron hybrids*—Flannel Bush		●	●			VF	●	●			●					●	7-24	T2,4 TS11,12,14, 15,17,18 GC6,8,9,11 P36
TS32 CN *Garrya elliptica*—Coast Silktassel		●	●		●	F	●	●	●	●					●	●	5-9 14-21	T2,13 TS3-5, 35 GC3,4,6,8, 9,11 P2 AB1,3
TS33 *Grevillea 'Canberra'*		●	●			F	●	●					●		●	●	8,9 12-24	T11,19 TS38,39 GC1,16,17 AB3 P19,25
TS34 *Grevillea rosmarinifolia*—Rosemary Grevillea		●				M	●	●			●				●	●	8,9 12-24	T34,36 TS22,39 SS10,15,18 V19,22 OG1 GC1,16,26 P15,47 AB5 B2
TS35 CN *Heteromeles arbutifolia*—Toyon		●	●		●	M	●	●	●				●			●	5-24	T2,53,55 TS11,12,14, 29 SS5 GC1,6 AB10 P29,49,50
TS36 *Ilex aquifolium*—English Holly		●			●	S-M	●	●		●		●	●		●	● ●	4-6 15-17	T24,49 TS7,38,45 SS1,5,12,13 V3,4 OG1,5 GC4,6,28 P1,2,8 AB13,18 B3,5,7

TS31 CN — Dark green 3" leaves may be hidden by the 3" golden flowers in spring for 30 days. Water first year, no summer water thereafter. Pinch new shoots monthly. *'California Glory', 'San Gabriel', 'Pacific Sunset'* superior forms. Fast to 20' tall. Best planted on a south or west facing slope in well-drained soil.

TS32 CN — A coarse plant 8' to 10' tall with 2" to 3" rounded, dark green, leathery leaves. In January to February, greenish-yellow male catkins are produced, often during rains which wash off the yellow pollen. *'James Roof'* is a leggy plant with 12" to 14" catkins. *'Evie'* is a more compact plant with 10" to 12" catkins. Should be pruned after blooming to improve shape.

TS33 — To 10' tall and 15' wide at maturity, to 6' tall by 10' wide in 3 years. Dark green needlelike foliage densely covers the plant. Clusters of 1" red, spiderlike flowers in spring. A good barrier plant. More tolerant of alkaline soil than most Grevilleas.

TS34 — A dense 4' to 5' tall dark green ball of 1" long narrow leaves. The undersides are white. Red and cream 1" flowers are scattered over the plant from fall through spring, providing winter hummingbird food. More tolerant of garden conditions than *Grevillea noelli.*

TS35 CN — A dark green mound in full light, semiopen and sprawling under Oaks where it appears naturally. Best in part shade. Usually 8' to 10' and as broad. The serrated leaves are 3" to 6" long. Clusters of white flowers in spring, and red fruit in fall. Lower branches should not be pruned off. Old plants may be rejuvenated by cutting to 2' tall in February.

TS36 — Slow growth when young, but eventually to 30', depending on cultivar used. Three-inch dark glossy green leaves are very spiny. Most cultivars become a densely foliaged pyramid. Male and female plants needed for berry set. Extremely drought tolerant once established. Will not tolerate alkaline soils.

TS31
Flannel
Bush

TS32
Coast
Silktassel

TS33
Grevillea
'Canberra'

TS34
Rosemary
Grevillea

TS35
Toyon

TS36
English
Holly

54

Tall Shrubs

	Important Characteristics						Cultural Preferences					Tolerances						Aesthetic and Cultural Compatibility
Plant name and description	Deciduous	Evergreen	Flowers	Fall Color	Fruit	Growth Rate	Full Sun	Part Shade	Well Drained Soil	Monthly Irrigation	No Water After 2nd Yr.	Alkaline Soil	Seacoast Conditions	Sprinklers	Wind	Heat	Sunset Zones	
TS37 *Ilex cornuta 'Burfordii'*—Burford Chinese Holly		•	•			M	•	•	•					•	•	•	8,9 14-16 18-21	T42,47 TS20,22,30 SS1,13 V10 OG4 GC16,26,28 P17,18 AB2,15 B6,12
TS38 *Juniperus chinensis 'Kaizuka'*—Hollywood Juniper		•				M	•	•	•	•			•	•	•	•	ALL	T46,52 TS39,59,67, 68 SS5 GC19,23
TS39 *Juniperus chinensis 'Mint Julep'*—Mint Julep Juniper		•				M	•	•	•	•			•	•	•	•	ALL	T46,51 TS38,65 GC9,23 P37
TS40 *Leonotis leonurus*—Lion's Tail		•	•			F	•		•	•		•			•	•	8-24	T54,56 TS24 SS6,7,8 GC6,11 P34,46,48, 49
TS41 *Leptospermum laevigatum*—Australian Tea Tree		•	•			M-S	•	•				•	•	•	•	•	14-24	T8,18,19 TS38,39,49 GC5,19,29 P22,28
TS42 *Leptospermum scoparium cultivars*—New Zealand Tea Tree		•	•			F	•		•	•		•		•	•	•	14-24	T35,37,38 TS38,39 SS5 GC1 P21,50,55

TS37 *Ilex cornuta 'Burfordii'*—Burford Chinese Holly

A 4' to 6' tall spreading shrub covered with glossy, medium green, 2-1/2" leaves with 5 spines per leaf; 1/2" red berries are scattered over the shrub in late summer through winter. Tolerant of a variety of soils, part shade or sun. Easily shaped.

TS38 *Juniperus chinensis 'Kaizuka'*—Hollywood Juniper

To 30' tall, 40' broad in old age. The twisted, irregular limbs are densely covered with rich green foliage. Easily pruned to any shape, from a formal hedge to a statuesque informal specimen. Should not be used within 10' of a structure.

TS39 *Juniperus chinensis 'Mint Julep'*—Mint Julep Juniper

A brilliant green, vase-shaped plant. To 3' tall, 6' spread with fine-textured, dense cover of foliage. More tolerant of water mold diseases than most. Easily sheared as hedge.

TS40 *Leonotis leonurus*—Lion's Tail

This South African shrub is upright in habit to 6' and as broad. Dark green 2" long leaves are complemented by the brilliant orange, 2" tubular flowers borne in clusters which surround the upper stems from midsummer to fall. Blends well with sages.

TS41 *Leptospermum laevigatum*—Australian Tea Tree

Can grow to 20', usually developing into a specimen with a twisted trunk which looks at home by the ocean. Attractive, peeling gray bark and 1/2" leaves. White, 1/2" flowers in spring. Tolerates most soils. An excellent formal or informal hedge.

TS42 *Leptospermum scoparium cultivars*—New Zealand Tea Tree

From a ground cover to 20' tall, depending on cultivar used. 'Ruby Glow' is 6' tall, with maroon foliage and double red flowers in late winter. 'Keatleyi' is semiopen to 15' tall, gray-green in foliage, 1" single pink flowers in spring. Needs water to get established.

TS37
Burford
Chinese
Holly

TS38
Hollywood
Juniper

TS39
Mint Julep
Juniper

TS40
Lion's
Tail

TS41
Australian
Tea Tree

TS42
New
Zealand
Tea Tree

Tall Shrubs

	Important Characteristics					Cultural Preferences					Tolerances					Sunset Zones	Aesthetic and Cultural Compatibility
Plant name and description	Deciduous	Evergreen	Flowers	Fall Color	Fruit	Growth Rate	Full Sun	Part Shade	Well Drained Soil	Monthly Irrigation	No Water After 2nd Yr.	Alkaline Soil	Seacoast Conditions	Sprinklers	Wind	Heat		
TS43 *Ligustrum japonicum, L. ovalifolium*—Japanese, California Privet		•	•	•		F	•	•			•				•	• •	4-24	T53,54,58 TS60 SS14 GC4,19 P4,37
TS44 CN *Mahonia aquifolium*—Oregon Holly Grape		•	•	•		M	•	•	•						•	• •	1-21	T4,9 TS70,71,72 GC19 P1,8,38 F1-4
TS45 CN *Mahonia pinnata*—California Holly Grape		•	•	•		M	•	•	•			•	•		•	• •	8,9 14-24	T55,58 TS11,12,14, 15,21,31 GC6,8,32
TS46 CN *Myrica californica*—Pacific Wax Myrtle		•				M	•	•	•			•	•	•	•	• •	8,9 14-17	T4,25,53 TS74,78 GC3,4,6 P1 AB18 F5,6
TS47 *Myrsine africanum*—African Box		•				M	•	•	•			•		•	•	• •	8,9 14-17	T14,16 TS69,76 GC16,17 P11,28 B7
TS48 *Myrtus communis*—Myrtle		•	•	•		M	•	•		•		•			•		•	8-24	T8,20 TS14 GC4,9,19 P28,33

TS43 — Evergreen or semideciduous shrubs to 30' tall. Used for hedges and screens. Japanese Privet has 3" to 5" long glossy evergreen foliage. It reseeds heavily in gardens and fruit is messy over walks. California Privet has 1-1/2" dark green foliage, is very drought and shade tolerant and does not reseed.

TS44 — Stiff, upright 3' to 6' shrub. Dark, shiny green hollylike leaflets create a coarse texture. Terminal clusters of bright yellow flowers in late spring. Bluish berries follow in fall. Needs Mahonia looper caterpillar control in May. Performs best in partial shade.

TS45 — Four to five feet tall and broad with vertical branches and spiny, dark green leaflets. Bright yellow, terminal flower spikes in spring with blue fruit clusters following. More drought and sun tolerant than *Mahonia aquifolium*.

TS46 — Up to 30' high but usually 8'. Used for screen or hedge. Glossy, light green leaves. Inconspicuous flowers and fruit. Some Red Spider Mite problems on unwatered specimens. May be trained as multistemmed tree.

TS47 — Vertical, wine red stems covered with dark green, glossy, round 1/2" leaves. To 5' tall if unpruned, or easily kept to 3' to 4' tall, 2' wide, if sheared two to three times per year. Shade, sun and alkaline soil tolerant.

TS48 — A dense, round form 5' to 8' tall, to 20' at maturity. Dark green, aromatic 1" leaves. White, fuzzy aromatic flowers in summer. Blue-black berries in fall. Shears well. M.c. *compacta* makes a dense, small foliaged pyramid or fine-textured hedge.

TS43
California Privet

TS44
Oregon Holly Grape

TS45
California Holly Grape

TS46
Pacific Wax Myrtle

TS47
African Box

TS48
Myrtle

Tall Shrubs

	Important Characteristics					Cultural Preferences				Tolerances								Aesthetic and Cultural Compatibility
Plant name and description	Deciduous	Evergreen	Flowers	Fall Color	Fruit	Growth Rate	Full Sun	Part Shade	Well Drained Soil	Monthly Irrigation	No Water After 2nd Yr.	Alkaline Soil	Seacoast Conditions	Sprinklers	Wind	Heat	Sunset Zones	

TS49 Nandina domestica—Heavenly Bamboo

Stiff, vertically branched shrubs with compound leaves of many 1" to 1-1/2" soft green leaflets, creating a lacy pattern. Fall color pink in shade to brilliant red in sun. *N.d. compacta* lacier texture, dense growth. *N.d. 'Royal Princess'* is fine-textured, semi-open, good fall color.

Characteristics: Flowers ●, Fall Color ●, Fruit ●, Growth Rate M, Full Sun ●, Part Shade ●, Well Drained Soil ●, Monthly Irrigation ●, Wind ●, Heat ●, Sunset Zones 5-24
Aesthetic and Cultural Compatibility: T24-26,28 TS3,44,51,57 SS14 GC24 P8,20,29 F2-6

TS50 Nerium oleander—Oleander

Depending on the cultivar, 4' to 15' tall. Dark green pointed 3" to 5" leaves fully cover plant. Fastest in hot climates. Heavy summer flowering in salmon, pink, red or white. White *'Sister Agnes'* is good background for blue flowers, or for *'Mrs. Roeding'*, double salmon. Semi-dwarf forms *'Tangier'* (pink). *'Casablanca'* (white) are half size.

Characteristics: Flowers ●, Fall Color ●, Growth Rate VF, Full Sun ●, Seacoast Conditions ●, Wind ●, Heat ●, (●), Sunset Zones 8-16, 18-23
Aesthetic and Cultural Compatibility: T15,20 TS11,19,59 SS5,6 GC6 B2,7

TS51 Osmanthus fragrans—Sweet Olive

Upright, branched stems with 3" to 4" glossy green spined leaves; this handsome shrub may reach 20' in reasonable soil. Best in part shade, but tolerant of sun if watered occasionally. Small, very fragrant white flowers are hidden. An elegant hedge.

Characteristics: Evergreen ●, Flowers ●, Growth Rate S-M, Full Sun ●, Part Shade ●, Monthly Irrigation ●, Alkaline Soil ●, Sprinklers ●, Wind ●, Heat ●, Sunset Zones 8,9 12-24
Aesthetic and Cultural Compatibility: T24,25,26, 28 TS44,45,49 SS14 GC3,4,13 B8,11 F4

TS52 Philadelphus virginalis—Mock Orange

Deciduous, stiffly upright branches with many short side branches which produce clusters of fragrant white flowers in spring. Leave room for the 6' wide fountain-like branching for best show. Remove 1/3 of oldest canes 12" from the ground when flowering is finished. *'Minn Snowflake'* has double flowers, *'Natchez'* single flowers to 7' tall.

Characteristics: Deciduous ●, Flowers ●, Growth Rate F, Full Sun ●, Part Shade ●, Well Drained Soil ●, Monthly Irrigation ●, Wind ●, Heat ●, Sunset Zones 1-17
Aesthetic and Cultural Compatibility: T57,62 TS8,47,49 SS3,14 V17,23 OG3 GC12,14,36 P11,13 AB13,16 B1,8

TS53 Phlomis fruticosa—Jerusalem Sage

A 3' coarse-textured, gray shrub topped by 2' to 3' of stiff, vertical branches. Ball-like clusters of 1" yellow flowers appear in whorls around these vertical shoots in early summer. Very drought tolerant once established.

Characteristics: Flowers ●, Fall Color ●, Growth Rate M, Full Sun ●, Well Drained Soil ●, Alkaline Soil ●, Sprinklers ●, Wind ●, Heat ●, (●), Sunset Zones ALL
Aesthetic and Cultural Compatibility: T48,52 TS12,40 SS2,10,18 V22 OG1 GC25,31,32 P24,32,37, 44,5 AB10,12,17 B1

TS54 Phormium tenax—New Zealand Flax

Swordlike, vertical leaves may be dark green, bronze, or maroon, or green and yellow striped. Green forms may become an 8' tall, 12' clump, most others smaller. Maroon flower on stalks above the foliage. Better with occasional water.

Characteristics: Flowers ●, Fall Color ●, Growth Rate F, Full Sun ●, Well Drained Soil ●, Alkaline Soil ●, Seacoast Conditions ●, Sprinklers ●, Wind ●, Heat ●, (●), Sunset Zones 7-24
Aesthetic and Cultural Compatibility: T50,64 TS38,39,58 GC1,16,19 AB6,8,10

TS49
Heavenly
Bamboo

TS50
Oleander

TS51
Sweet Olive

TS52
Mock
Orange

TS53
Jerusalem
Sage

TS54
New
Zealand
Flax

Tall Shrubs

	Important Characteristics				Cultural Preferences				Tolerances								
Plant name and description	Evergreen Deciduous	Flowers	Fall Color	Fruit	Growth Rate	Full Sun	Part Shade	Well Drained Soil	Monthly Irrigation	No Water After 2nd Yr.	Alkaline Soil	Seacoast Conditions	Sprinklers	Wind	Heat	Sunset Zones	Aesthetic and Cultural Compatibility
TS55 *Photinia fraseri*—Fraser Photinia	●	●			F	●		●	●	●	●			●		4-16 18-22	T48 TS1,67,74 SS5 P20,44
TS56 *Photinia serrulata*—Chinese Photinia	●	●	●		M	●	●		●				●	●	●	4-24	T24,46 TS57,68 GC4 P20,44
TS57 *Phyllostachys aurea*—Golden Bamboo	●				VF	●	●		●		●	●		●	●	●	4-24	T4,45 TS3 SS14 GC23 P4,5
TS58 *Pittosporum eugenioides, Pittosporum tenuifolium*	●				M	●	●	●	●				●	●	●	9 14-17 19-22	T30,43 TS6,7,59 SS1,5,14 P28,32,37
TS59 *Plumbago auriculata*—Cape Plumbago *(Plumbago capensis)*	●	●			M	●	●		●					●		8,9 12-24	T20,27 TS50,51,58, 60 GC6,11 P43,57
TS60 *Podocarpus macrophylla*—Yew Pine	●				S	●	●		●				●	●		4-9 12-24	T41,45 TS59,67,68, 69 SS3 GC3,4,32 P8,20

TS55 *Photinia fraseri*—Fraser Photinia

The bright red foliaged shrub used along highways. It can become a 20' tree, but is easily kept at 5' tall with frequent pruning. 6" clusters of white flowers appear in spring if unpruned in fall. Foliage turns yellow and may drop off in wet clay soils.

TS56 *Photinia serrulata*—Chinese Photinia

Grows in full sun or light shade to 20' tall. Saw-toothed, 6" leaves are reddish bronze when new. Small white flowers borne in flat clusters in spring. Bright red berries. Mildews in areas of part shade or poor air circulation.

TS57 *Phyllostachys aurea*—Golden Bamboo

Yellowish 10' to 20' canes to 1-1/2" diameter, gracefully covered with soft green 2" to 3" leaves. Can be extremely invasive and messy, dropping leaves year round. In the right place, is unsurpassed as tall screen. Tolerant of drought, better with some water.

TS58 *Pittosporum eugenioides, Pittosporum tenuifolium*

Vertical branches to 40' tall in old age. Usually used as a 10' to 20' screen or trimmed hedge. *Pittosporum eugenioides* has 2", wavy-edged, yellow green leaves. *Pittosporum tenuifolium* has 1-1/2", pale lime green leaves with black twigs. Good as small trees.

TS59 *Plumbago auriculata*—Cape Plumbago *(Plumbago capensis)*

Arching branches to 6' high with 10' spread or larger. Light green, 1-1/2" leaves. Intense light blue or white flowers in 3" to 4" clusters in summer. Tender at 20°F. Prefers full sun, but flowers in part shade. Easily kept at 3' tall.

TS60 *Podocarpus macrophylla*—Yew Pine

Usually used as trimmed shrub to 10', it will make an asymmetrical 20' to 30' tree in old age. Easily pruned to any shape. Dark olive green in east or north exposures, more yellow in sun. Elegant sheared hedge, handsome smooth gray bark.

TS55
Fraser
Photinia

TS56
Chinese
Photinia

TS57
Golden
Bamboo

TS58
Pittosporum
eugenioides

TS59
Cape
Plumbago

TS60
Yew Pine

62

Tall Shrubs

	Important Characteristics					Cultural Preferences			Tolerances								Sunset Zones	Aesthetic and Cultural Compatibility
Plant name and description	Deciduous	Evergreen	Flowers	Fruit	Fall Color	Growth Rate	Full Sun	Part Shade	Well Drained Soil	Monthly Irrigation	No Water After 2nd Yr.	Alkaline Soil	Seacoast Conditions	Sprinklers	Wind	Heat		
TS61 *Prostanthera rotundifolia*—Mint Bush			•	•		F	•	•		•						•	8,9 14-24	T2,52 TS11,14,20 SS2,7,10 V20,22 OG2 GC30,31,33 P14,22,23 AB10,12 B2,10
TS62 *Prunus caroliniana*—Carolina Laurel Cherry		•	•	•		F	•	•	•					•		•	7-24	T53 TS44,63 GC29 P21,37
TS63 CN *P. illicifolia, P. lyonii*—Holly-Leaf, Catalina Cherry		•	•	•		M	•	•	•		•		•	•	•	•	7-9 12-24	T53 TS11,12,14,15,59,62 GC8,9,11,29
TS64 *Prunus lusitanica*—Portugal Laurel		•	•	•		S-M	•	•	•					•		•	4-9 14-24	T24,53 TS1,6 SS5 P4
TS65 *Punica granatum 'Wonderful'*—Pomegranate		•	•	•		S-M	•	•					•			•	4-24	T53,55,56 TS1,35,44 GC3,4,8,28
TS66 *Rhamnus californica*—California Coffeeberry	•		•	•	•	F	•		•		•	•		•	•	•	7-24	T11,53,56 TS3,45 SS1 GC1,23

TS61 *Prostanthera rotundifolia*—Mint Bush

The vertical branches arch as they reach 4' to 6' of height. Covered with 1/2" round leaves which smell like mint when brushed. During April and May, the plant is hidden by rose pink, lavender or purple 1/2" flowers in a psychedelic display. Must have good drainage.

TS62 *Prunus caroliniana*—Carolina Laurel Cherry

Fast growing to 12' to 20' high with dense, pyramidal habit. Shiny, yellow-green 2" leaves. Small purple-black berries. Needs some water. Can reseed in garden. Susceptible to Flat Head Borer insects. Avoid bark injury. Resistant to Oak Root fungus.

TS63 CN *P. illicifolia, P. lyonii*—Holly-Leaf, Catalina Cherry

A large shrub or small tree to 15'. Whitish flowers in 3" panacles in March. Purple 1" fruit in fall resembles cherries, can be messy. Tolerates part shade. Oak root fungus resistant. *P. illicifolia* has glossy green 1-1/2" leaves, spiny edged; *P. lyonii* has 3" leaves, smooth margins.

TS64 *Prunus lusitanica*—Portugal Laurel

Forms a dark green densely foliaged mass 6' to 15' tall. Glossy 4" leaves with toothed margins. White flowers in showy 10" racemes in May. Small purple berries in summer. Slow growth rate and some scale problems are drawbacks. Needs monthly water to establish.

TS65 *Punica granatum 'Wonderful'*—Pomegranate

A fountain-shaped shrub to 10' with narrow 2" yellow-green leaves on a twiggy structure. Orange-red 2" to 4" flowers in summer can be spectacular. Fruit not produced in coastal areas. Deep watering monthly is necessary if fruit is desired.

TS66 *Rhamnus californica*—California Coffeeberry

An upright or spreading habit from 3' to 15' tall. Dark green leaves with pale undersides on red stems; 1/2" berries turn from green to red to black. The compact 'Eve Case' is 4' to 6' with broader foliage and heavier fruiting. Excellent under old Oaks.

TS61
Mint Bush

TS62
Carolina
Laurel
Cherry

TS63
Catalina
Cherry

TS64
Portugal
Laurel

TS65
Pome-
granate

TS66
*Rhamnus
californica
'Eve
Case'*

64

Tall Shrubs

Column headers (left to right): Deciduous, Evergreen, Flowers, Fall Color, Fruit | Growth Rate, Full Sun, Part Shade | Well Drained Soil, Monthly Irrigation, No Water After 2nd Yr., Alkaline Soil, Seacoast Conditions, Sprinklers, Wind, Heat | Sunset Zones | Aesthetic and Cultural Compatibility

TS67 — *Rhaphiolepis indica*—India Hawthorn

Flowers · Fall Color; Growth Rate M; Full Sun; Well Drained Soil · Alkaline Soil · Seacoast Conditions; Sprinklers · Wind · Heat; Sunset Zones 8-10, 12-24; Compatibility T53,54,55 TS51,64,68 SS5

From 12' to 14' tall, 3' to 8' spread depending on cultivar. Glossy, pointed 2" to 3" leaves. Most trustworthy in heavy soils are 'Snow White' at 3' tall, 4' to 5' spread, white flowers, and 'Springtime' at 4' to 5' tall, 6' to 8' spread, bright pink flowers.

TS68 — *Rhaphiolepis umbellata*—Yeddo Hawthorn

Flowers · Fall Color; Growth Rate M; Full Sun · Part Shade · Well Drained Soil · Monthly Irrigation; Alkaline Soil · Seacoast Conditions · Sprinklers · Wind · Heat; Sunset Zones 8-10, 12-24; Compatibility T10,53,58 TS67 SS9,14,17 GC23,24

Round-tipped dark green 2" to 3" leaves are dusted with white powder. Old plants may be 8' tall, 12' across, but easily kept at 4' to 6' tall by annual pruning. White flowers in clusters in spring. More tolerant of heavy clay soils than *R. indica*.

TS69 CN — *Rhus integrifolia*—Lemonade Berry

Flowers · Fall Color · Fruit; Growth Rate M; Full Sun · Part Shade · Well Drained Soil · Monthly Irrigation; Alkaline Soil · Seacoast Conditions · Sprinklers · Wind · Heat; Sunset Zones 15-17; Compatibility T2,4,57 OG1,6

A rounded shrub of 4' to 10' with 2" round glossy green leaves. A useful massive background plant in the dry garden. Light pink flowers in clusters in early spring. Shear to hedge if desired. Better with occasional water.

TS70 CN — *Ribes sanguineum*—Flowering Currant

Deciduous; Flowers; Growth Rate M; Full Sun · Part Shade; Heat; Sunset Zones 4-9, 14-24; Compatibility T53,55,56, 62 TS35,46,49, 63,66 GC3,4,28 P8,29 AB7

Stiff, upright habit 3' to 12' tall. Light green, hairy, maple-shaped leaves. Dense 3" clusters of dark pink flowers all winter an early spring are attractive to hummingbirds. Black berries in later summer. Grow in part shade or sun. Must have good air movement to avoid white fly problems. White flowered forms available.

TS71 CN — *Ribes speciosum*—Fuchsia-Flowered Gooseberry

Deciduous; Flowers · Fall Color; Growth Rate M; Full Sun · Part Shade · Well Drained Soil; Heat; Sunset Zones 8,9, 14-24; Compatibility T52,54 TS4,10,13,14 SS9,13 V19,22 OG1,4 GC3,4,6,28 P1,8,19 AB4,10,18 B1,5

Nearly evergreen 3' to 6' shrub for use under the canopy of trees. Spiny branches with rows of shiny, rounded 1" leaves. In spring, small red tubular flowers hang in rows from branches. Pruned canes often die to ground.

TS72 — *Sarcoccoca ruscifolia*—Fragrant Sarcoccoca

Flowers · Fall Color · Fruit; Growth Rate S-M; Part Shade; Wind; Sunset Zones 14-24; Compatibility T9,14 TS1,3,51 SS14 GC3,4,13,30 P4,8,20,21

To 4' to 6' with age, usually 2' to 3' tall, composed of bright green shoots from the ground, semiclothed with dark, glossy green 1-1/2" leaves. In spring, hidden white flowers lend fragrance. Will tolerate deep shade. Drought tolerant after three to four years.

TS67
India
Hawthorn

TS68
Yeddo
Hawthorn

TS69
Lemonade
Berry

TS70
Ribes
sanguineum
glutinosum

TS71
Fuchsia-
Flowered
Gooseberry

TS72
Fragrant
Sarcoc-
coca

Tall Shrubs

Plant name and description	Deciduous	Evergreen	Flowers	Fall Color	Fruit	Growth Rate	Full Sun	Part Shade	Well Drained Soil	Monthly Irrigation	No Water After 2nd Yr.	Alkaline Soil	Seacoast Conditions	Sprinklers	Wind	Heat	Sunset Zones	Aesthetic and Cultural Compatibility
TS73 *Syringa vulgaris*—Lilac	•		•			S	•	•		•		•				•	1-12 14-16 18-22	T24,38,57 TS1,6,26 SS9,16 V7,12 OG1 GC20,28 P27,30,32 AB18 B1,2,5
TS74 *Syzygium paniculatum*—Australian Brush Cherry		•	•		•	F	•	•	•	•		•		•	•	• •	16-17 19-24	T4,14,25 TS5,44,51 SS14 GC3,4 AB6,8
TS75 *Tecomaria capensis*—Cape Honeysuckle		•	•			VF	•							•	•	•	12-13 16 18-24	T17,61 TS11,12,14, 40,56 GC16,17,23, 24 P50
TS76 *Viburnum suspensum*—Sandankwa Viburnum		•				M		•	•			•			•	•	15-24	T14,24 TS47,48,49, 68 SS14 P1,8
TS77 *Viburnum tinus*—Laurestinus		•	•			M-F	•	•	•	•		•			•	•	14-23	T26,31,52 TS58,59 GC15,17,19 P11 F1
TS78 *Xylosma congestum*—Shiny Xylosma		•				F	•		•			•		•	•	•	8-24	T30,61,64 TS23,69 GC6 P22,32

TS73 *Syringa vulgaris*—Lilac

May reach 15' with age, but commonly kept to 6' tall. The old varieties may not flower well in zones 16, 17. Plant in the coldest part of the garden in full sun or part shade, but with good air movement. 8' to 12' tall spikes of intensely fragrant flowers of white, pink, lavender or purple appear in late March to late May.

TS74 *Syzygium paniculatum*—Australian Brush Cherry

A tall, narrow plant thickly covered with 2" dark green leaves which are hidden by the bright red new foliage. Excellent as a corner speciment o 30' tall, 8' diameter, or a clipped hedge. If badly frozen, quickly resprouts; 1" white flowers in late spring.

TS75 *Tecomaria capensis*—Cape Honeysuckle

Used as a bank cover, espalier or hedge up to 15' to 25'. Shiny, dark green, compound leaves will cover densely if sheared. Orange-red 3" flower clusters October to winter. Tolerates salt spray. May be damaged at 22°F, but recoves quickly.

TS76 *Viburnum suspensum*—Sandankwa Viburnum

Oval 3" leaves of dark leathery green. To 8' to 10' tall if unpruned, but easily kept at 3' with shearing. Flowers are white, but inconspicuous. A good filler in part or deep shade. Aphids and White Fly are a problem without good air movement.

TS77 *Viburnum tinus*—Laurestinus

From 3' to 20' tall, depending on cultivar. Three inch long oval leaves of dark green on vertical stems topped in late winter with white flowers in 2" to 3" clusters. Mildews in shade. *V.t. 'Robustum'* is tall, with larger leaves, more resistant to mildew. *'Spring Bouquet'* more compact, to 6' tall. May produce a musty smell.

TS78 *Xylosma congestum*—Shiny Xylosma

Can be espaliered, sheared or trained into a small multi-stemmed tree 10' to 20' tall. Golden-green, 1-1/2" leaves are tinted bronze when new. Tolerates desert conditions. *X.c. 'Compacta'* to 3' tall, dense habit, with some spines.

TS73
Lilac

TS74
Australian
Brush
Cherry

TS75
Cape
Honey-
suckle

TS76
Sandankwa
Viburnum

TS77
Laurestinus

TS78
Shiny
Xylosma

68

Short Shrubs

	Important Characteristics				Cultural Preferences				Tolerances								Aesthetic and Cultural Compatibility
	Deciduous	Evergreen	Flowers	Fall Color	Fruit	Growth Rate	Well Drained Soil	Part Shade	Full Sun	No Water After 2nd Yr	Monthly Irrigation	Seacoast Conditions	Alkaline Soil	Sprinklers	Wind	Heat	Sunset Zones	
SS1 *Buxus microphylla japonica*—Japanese Boxwood		●				S	●		●			●		●	●	●	8-24	T53,55 TS1,9,16, 50,65 SS1,16 V8,21 OG5` GC26,27 P28,33 AB16,17 B6,7
SS2 *Cistus skanbergii*—Hybrid Rockrose		●	●			F	●	●	●	●	●	●	●		●	●	best 16,17	T4,42,43 TS32 GC6,15 P4,34,57, 60 AB10
SS3 *Correa 'Carmine Bells'*—Australian Fuchsia		●	●			S-M	●	●	●	●					●	●	14-24	T53-56 TS38,51
SS4 *Correa 'Ivory Bells'*—Australian Fuchsia		●	●			M	●	●	●	●						●	14-24	T57,58 TS2,41 SS18 V20 OG2,6 GC2,31 P22,26 AB12,13 B9,12
SS5 *Cotoneaster congesta 'Likiang'*—Likiang Cotoneaster		●	●	●		M	●			●					●	●	2-24	T6,7 TS3-5 GC6 P16,57
SS6 *Cytisus kewensis*—Kew Broom		●	●			M	●		●	●						●	4-6 best, 16-17	T6,7 TS11,12,14, 68,69 GC6,29 P32,36

Plant name and description

SS1 *Buxus microphylla japonica*—Japanese Boxwood

Naturally forms a 4' ball of bright, shiny yellow-green 1/2" foliage but can be sheared to a 12" hedge. Unpruned it can provide a tough background planting. Tolerates sun, part shade and alkaline soil. *'Green Beauty'* and *'Winter Gem'* retain green color during winter.

SS2 *Cistus skanbergii*—Hybrid Rockrose

A 1-1/2' to 3' tall, 4' to 6' broad mound of gray-green, narrow foliage. Needs monthly watering and annual shearing to be its best. Covered with 1" light pink flowers in spring.

SS3 *Correa 'Carmine Bells'*—Australian Fuchsia

A dense spreading habit to 3' tall by 6'. The 1" leaves are dark green above, pale green below. Pendulous 1" carmine red bells are borne August to March. Very attractive to hummingbirds. *Must* have good drainage. Deer resistant.

SS4 *Correa 'Ivory Bells'*—Australian Fuchsia

A rounded form to 3' tall and as wide. The 1-1/2" round gray-green leaves and twigs are an excellent background for the 1" tubular cream-colored flowers. These appear evenly through the year. Excellent winter food for hummingbirds. Deer resistant.

SS5 *Cotoneaster congesta 'Likiang'*—Likiang Cotoneaster

Low rounded shrub 18" to 2' with arching branches and small, dark green foliage. 1/2" white flowers in spring, small red berries in fall. Slower growing than *Cotoneaster 'Lowfast'*, better for smaller areas.

SS6 *Cytisus kewensis*—Kew Broom

A cover 8" to 1' tall with a 4' spread. A dense pad of tiny leaves on bright green twigs. Covered with creamy white flowers April to May. Does not reseed.

SS1
Japanese
Boxwood

SS2
Hybrid
Rockrose

SS3
Australian
Fuchsia

SS4
Australian
Fuchsia

SS5
Likiang
Cotoneaster

SS6
Kew
Broom

Short Shrubs

	Plant name and description	Deciduous	Evergreen	Flowers	Fall Color	Fruit	Growth Rate	Full Sun	Part Shade	Well Drained Soil	Monthly Irrigation	No Water After 2nd Yr.	Alkaline Soil	Seacoast Conditions	Sprinklers	Wind	Heat	Sunset Zones	Aesthetic and Cultural Compatibility
SS7 CN	***Eriogonum crocatum*—Saffron Buckwheat** A compact 18" mound of white, woolly leaves and stems. The 1" round leaves have wavy edges. Brilliant yellow 4" flower clusters are borne on 4" stems above the foliage from April to August.		●	●			F	●		●		●		●		●	● ●	14-24	T6 TS2,23-25 SS2,8 GC9,11,15
SS8 CN	***Eriogonum umbellatum polyanthum*—Sulfur Buckwheat** Gray-green 1" leaves cover this easy, low mounding border plant which grows 8" tall with a 3' spread. Bright yellow flower heads are held 4" above the foliage in spring, then dry on the plant, remaining attractive. Very cold tolerant.		●	●			F	●	●	●		●			●	●	●	ALL	T6 TS2,23 SS2 GC11,13,15 P43
SS9	***Escallonia Dwarf Forms*** Dark green, glossy 1-1/2" leaves cover these compact, rounded shrubs. New growth is lighter green. 'Newport Dwarf' is 3' tall, with carmine red flowers much of the year. 'Terri' matures at 4' tall, with a 6' spread. Pink flowers in spring and fall.		●	●			M	●	●	●	●		●		●	●	●	14-17	T16,30 TS26,47 GC16,17 P4,6,20
SS10	***Grevillea lanigera*—Woolly Grevillea** Mounding plant of 3' to 5' tall, 6' broad; 1/2" gray-green foliage densely covers plant. Red and creme flowers scattered profusely through the plant, attracting hummingbirds. Tolerant of heat and drought once established.		●	●			M	●		●		●				●	●	15-24	T6,7,38 TS33,41,61 SS2,4,18 V12,20 OG2,3 GC1,13,30, 35 P3,6,7,12,31 AB4,5 B1,6
SS11	***Ilex cornuta rotunda*—Dwarf Chinese Holly** A 1-1/2' tall, 3' wide neatly rounded shrub, densely covered with 2-1/2" long medium green glossy leaves, tipped by 3 stout spines. This very spiny shrub makes a good foreground for stone walls and a good barrier plant. Brittle if stepped on. Doesn't shear well, nor does it need it. Tolerant of many soils unless overwet.		●		●		M	●	●		●				●	●	●	8,9 14-16 18-21	T52,55,58, 63 TS60,62,76 SS13,17 V2,7,8 OG6 GC16,17,32 P16,37,52 AB2 B4,8
SS12	***Ilex vomitoria 'Nana'*—Dwarf Yaupon** An 18" tall ball of 3/4" bright green, narrow leaves. An excellent hedge or filler, sheared or natural. May produce quantities of tiny red berries. Tolerant of highly alkaline soils. Full sun in zones 16, 17, part shade in zones 14, 15.		●				S	●	●			●			●	●	●	3-9 11-24	T62,63 TS69,78 SS5 V10,13 OG1 GC14,16 P52,56 AB13,15 B3,9

SS7
Saffron
Buckwheat

SS8
Sulfur
Buckwheat

SS9
Dwarf
Escallonia

SS10
Woolly
Grevillea

SS11
Dwarf
Chinese
Holly

SS12
Dwarf
Yaupon

Short Shrubs

	Important Characteristics					Cultural Preferences			Tolerances								
Plant name and description	Evergreen Deciduous	Flowers	Fall Color	Fruit	Growth Rate	Full Sun	Part Shade	Well Drained Soil	Monthly Irrigation	No Water After 2nd Yr.	Alkaline Soil	Seacoast Conditions	Sprinklers	Wind	Heat	Sunset Zones	Aesthetic and Cultural Compatibility
SS13 CN *Mahonia aquifolium 'Compacta'*—Compact Oregon Grape	●				M		●						●	●	●	1-21	T53-56,62 TS1,5 SS1 GC18 P40
SS14 *Nandina domestica cultivars*—Heavenly Bamboo	●			●	M	●	●	●	●				●	●	●	5-24	T9,13,17 TS44,49,72 GC13,17,24 P8,42,43
SS15 *Pinus mugo*—Swiss Mountain Pine	●				S	●	●	●	●				●	●	●	ALL	T3,40,44 TS6,7,43 SS7,9 V9 OG1 GC8,13,23 P23,31 AB3,12,13 B3,7
SS16 *Punica granatum 'Nana'*—Dwarf Pomegranate	●	●	●		S	●				●		●	●	●	● ●	7-24	T29,49,53 TS37,47,60 SS11 V8 OG5 GC4,14,32 P32,56 AB17 B8
SS17 *Sollya heterophylla*—Australian Bluebell	●	●	●		S-M	●	●	●					●	●		8,9 14-24	T9,20,21, 23 TS29,35,51, 66 SS5 GC4,13 P8,20
SS18 *Westringia rosmariniformis*—Rosemary Bush Westringia	●	●			F	●		●					●	●	●	15-17 19-24	T37 TS2,28 GC11,29,34 P4,33,57,59

SS13 CN *Mahonia aquifolium 'Compacta'*—Compact Oregon Grape

Glossy, dark green, 2-1/2", spiny leaflets emerge from stiff, upright stems. If unpruned, these stems may become 2 feet tall and unattractive. Plant spreads by underground stems, forming a solid groundcover in well prepared soil with mulch. Prune off tallest stems in spring. Treat for Barberry Looper Caterpillar in May.

SS14 *Nandina domestica cultivars*—Heavenly Bamboo

Several cultivars make good low shrubs, 1' to 1-1/2' tall.. *N.d. 'Harbour Dwarf'* and *'Woods Dwarf'* have normal foliage, red fall color, spreading habit. *N.d. 'Purpurea '* has cupped, twisted leaflets, purple and green in summer, purplish in winter, non-spreading habit.

SS15 *Pinus mugo*—Swiss Mountain Pine

May be maintained as a 3' tall, dense dark green boulder substitute with annual spring pinching. Water as often as necessary to establish, then is very drought tolerant. Check for white specks on base of needles. Treat these Pine Adelgid as for aphids.

SS16 *Punica granatum 'Nana'*—Dwarf Pomegranate

A dense ball of 1-1/2" long, narrow, bright green leaves. New growth bronze. To 3' tall with age. Evergreen in mild winters, otherwise deciduous. Orange-red single 1-1/2" flowers begin appearing in summer of 3rd or 4th year. Tolerant of highly alkaline soil and heat but not of constantly wet soil.

SS17 *Sollya heterophylla*—Australian Bluebell

A neat 18" to 2' mound of bright green 1" leaves. During most of the summer, it produces 1/2" bright blue bells and follows with 3/4" purple beadlike fruit. Best in half shade. Grows well under Eucalyptus.

SS18 *Westringia rosmariniformis*—Rosemary Bush Westringia

Can be espaliered, sheared or trained into a small multi-stemmed tree 10' to 20' tall. Golden-green, 1-1/2' leaves are tinted bronze when new. Tolerates desert conditions. *W.r. 'Compacta'* to 3' tall, dense habit, with some spines.

SS13
Compact
Oregon
Grape

SS14
Heavenly
Bamboo

SS15
Swiss
Mountain
Pine

SS16
Dwarf
Pome-
granate

SS17
Australian
Bluebell

SS18
Rosemary
Bush
Westringia

74

Vines

	Plant name and description	Deciduous	Evergreen	Flowers	Fall Color	Fruit	Growth Rate	Full Sun	Part Shade	Well Drained Soil	Monthly Irrigation	No Water After 2nd Yr.	Alkaline Soil	Seacoast Conditions	Sprinklers	Wind	Heat	Sunset Zones	Aesthetic and Cultural Compatibility
V1	***Bougainvillea species***	•	•				S-F	•		•		•		• •			•	frost gamble 15-16 ok 17	T16,17,39, 60 TS29 GC1,16 P5
V2	***Campsis radicans*—Trumpet Creeper**	•	•				VF	•				•		• •	•			1-21	T20,27 TS23,62 GC6,23
V3	***Cissus antarctica*—Kangaroo Ivy**		•				F	• •		•	• •	• •	• •	•				16-24	T53-57 TS3,39 SS5,9,15 OG5
V4	***Clematis armandii*—Evergreen Clematis**		•	•			F	• •	•			•		•				4-6 15-17	T24,25 TS3,38 SS11,12 GC13,18 P4,20 B5
V5	***Clytostoma callistegioides*—Lavender Trumpet Vine**		•	•			S-F	• • • •				•		•				13-24	TS67,74 SS5,14,17 GC9,29
V6	***Disticus buccinatoria*—Blood Red Trumpet Vine**		•	•			S-F	• • •		•		• • •	•					8-9 14-24	T2,27,53 TS47,48,78 SS14 GC29

V1 ***Bougainvillea species***

Shrubby vines with 2" to 4" heart-shaped leaves. Very fast growth once established, but may take two years to establish. Water frequently during that time. Flower bracts are brilliant reds, as *'San Diego Red'*, purple as *B. specta-bilis*, or bluish-red, as *'Barbara Karst'*. Lighter colored forms are more frost sensitive.

V2 ***Campsis radicans*—Trumpet Creeper**

A deciduous rampant vine with dark green, compound leaves. Tubular, orange-red, 2" trumpet-shaped flowers August to September. Must be watered until established, then quite drought tolerant. Needs stout support.

V3 ***Cissus antarctica*—Kangaroo Ivy**

Among the toughest of vines. Tolerant of heat, severe drought and clay soils. Dark green foliage is 3 parted when young, 3" long, 2" wide on older plants. Tolerant of 18°F once established. Use it to cover fences or as a groundcover on a steep bank.

V4 ***Clematis armandii*—Evergreen Clematis**

These 6" long leaves are composed of three 5" hard, glossy green leaflets. They hang like shingles overlapping each other forming a beautiful pattern of woody vines which must be thinned every few years. The 1" white, intensely fragrant flowers appear in March-April. Plant with roots in shade.

V5 ***Clytostoma callistegioides*—Lavender Trumpet Vine**

Best with its roots in shade. Glossy green leaflets hang in a curtain. Tubular 3" lavender flowers can cover the vine in late spring, then bloom sporadically until fall. Very vigorous after established. Fertilize in late winter. Needs support.

V6 ***Disticus buccinatoria*—Blood Red Trumpet Vine**

Leaflets are medium green, 2" to 3" long and stand out at angles from the stem. Flowers appear in clusters throughout summer in response to hot spells. They are brilliant orange, red, fading to paler orange with a yellow throat. Prune in fall. Needs support.

V1
Bougainvil-
lea

V2
Trumpet
Creeper

V3
Kangaroo
Ivy

V4
Evergreen
Clematis

V5
Lavender
Trumpet
Vine

V6
Blood Red
Trumpet
Vine

76

Vines

Plant name and description	Evergreen/Deciduous	Flowers	Fall Color	Fruit	Growth Rate	Full Sun	Part Shade	Well Drained Soil	Monthly Irrigation	No Water After 2nd Yr.	Alkaline Soil	Seacoast Conditions	Sprinklers	Wind	Heat	Sunset Zones	Aesthetic and Cultural Compatibility
V7 *Euonymus fortunei radicans*—Common Wintercreeper Lush green, leathery 1-1/2" rounded leaves are spaced along the green vines. Many vining branches overlap to form a dense groundcover or wall cover. A better performer in poor soils than Ivy. Many variegated forms available.	●				F	●	●	●			●		●	●	●	1-17	T31,57 TS28,60 SS16,65 V10 OG3 GC28 P3 AB7,13 B2,7,11
V8 *Gelsemium sempervirens*—Carolina Jessamine Clean, shiny, medium green 2" leaves on hanging branches form a semiopen screen on a fence. Fragrant, tubular yellow 1" flowers appear in late winter and early spring. Tolerates sun or shade, blooms poorly in shade. Poisonous if eaten. Needs support.	●	●			M	●	●	●					●	●	●	8-24	T30,31 TS55 GC1,8
V9 *Hardenbergia violacea* 'Happy Wanderer' Four inch long, dark glossy green leaves completely cover this shrubby vine. Plant in a stump or against a fence. The purple, pendulous 4" flower clusters are mindful of Wisteria. This cultivar is drought and sun tolerant.	●	●			M	●	●	●					●	●	●	9-24	T48,61 TS51 SS3,17 GC31,35 P33,55 AB3 B11,12
V10 *Hibbertia scandens*—Guinea Gold Vine Dark green, succulent 3" leaves make a dense cover in deep shade or sun. May sunburn in full sun if not well watered. Drought tolerant in shade. Yellow 2-1/2" flowers like single roses from May to October. Needs support.	●	●			M		●	●					●	●	●	16-17 21-24	T19,49 TS38,44,76 SS14
V11 *Jasminum polyanthum*—Pink Jasmine Dark glossy green, divided foliage covers the pendulous branches. The intensely fragrant flowers may completely hide foliage in spring. Flowers are wine red in bud, opening to white. Best performance is on a west wall with roots shaded by a shrub.	●	●			M	●		●		●			●		●	12-24	T13 TS1,48,49 SS3,14
V12 *Lonicera hildebrandiana*—Giant Burmese Honeysuckle A giant version of other Honeysuckles. Dark green 6" glossy leaves and 4" long flowers of cream turning gold in clusters of 6 to 10. Fragrance may be overwhelming if planted too close to the house. Needs strong support, monthly watering.	●	●			F	●		●					●	●	●	9 14-17 19-24	T24-26 TS3,56 GC16

V7
Common
Winter-
creeper

V8
Carolina
Jessamine

V9
Harden-
bergia
violacea

V10
Guinea
Gold Vine

V11
Pink
Jasmine

V12
Giant
Burmese
Honey-
suckle

Vines

	Important Characteristics					Cultural Preferences				Tolerances								Aesthetic and Cultural Compatibility
Plant name and description	Deciduous	Evergreen	Flowers	Fall Color	Fruit	Growth Rate	Full Sun	Part Shade	Well Drained Soil	Monthly Irrigation	No Water After 2nd Yr	Alkaline Soil	Seacoast Conditions	Sprinklers	Wind	Heat	Sunset Zones	
V13 *Lonicera sempervirens*—Trumpet Honeysuckle	●		●		●	F	●				●			●	●	●	3-24	T61 TS72,77 SS5 OG1 GC36 P21,28 AB4,12 B1
V14 *Macfadyena unguis-cati*—Cat's Claw	●		●		●	VF	●					●		●	●	●	8-24	T8,11,29 TS45,59 GC8,9,19 P42
V15 *Muelenbeckia complexa*—Mattress Vine		●				M	●	●		●		●		●	●	●	8,9 14-24	T47 TS55,78 SS1,3 V21 OG3 GC6,33 P1,20 AB15 B5,12
V16 *Parthenocissus tricuspidata*—Boston Ivy	●			●		VF	●	●		●	●	●	●	●	●	●	ALL	T28,30 TS44,47 GC17 P1
V17 *Passiflora caerulea*—Passion Vine		●	●			M-F	●	●	●					●	●		12-24	T52 TS1,72,76 SS5 P38 AB7
V18 *Polygonum aubertii*—Silver Lace Vine	●	●				F	●				●			●	●	●	8,9 13-24	T19,29 TS11,12,14 GC29 P48

V13 *Lonicera sempervirens*—Trumpet Honeysuckle

A shrubby vine lightly covered by 2" glossy green leaves. Unscented 2" orange-yellow or red tubular flowers appear at the tips of the graceful vines in summer, followed by salmon-egg-like fruit.

V14 *Macfadyena unguis-cati*—Cat's Claw

Partly deciduous vine with growth rate related to the amount of heat it receives. Glossy green 2" leaflets. Yellow 2" trumpets cover vines in spring. Very aggressive climber on any surface, attaching itself with hold-fast "claws".

V15 *Muelenbeckia complexa*—Mattress Vine

A dense mattress of thin black stems densely covered by 1/2" round dark green leaves, this is the ideal cover for any ugly wall or junk heap. Inconspicuous flowers are followed by 3/4" white fruit. Indestructible once established. Dangerously invasive if not controlled. Good background for sculpture.

V16 *Parthenocissus tricuspidata*—Boston Ivy

Mature 6" to 8" leaves are three-lobed, medium green and held on long leaf stems, giving a "shingled" appearance. Fall color is brilliant red orange. *P.t. 'Vietchii'* has smaller foliage, new growth purple. Climbs by "feet" on any surface. Alkaline soil tolerant.

V17 *Passiflora caerulea*—Passion Vine

The attractive three-lobed, 3" medium green leaves may drop in a very cold winter, but will regrow. Fragrant 3-1/2" flowers are white, pink and lavender with deep blue centers, appearing all summer. Not fruit producing. Best out of afternoon sun and wind.

V18 *Polygonum aubertii*—Silver Lace Vine

Fast growing to invasive. Semideciduous in colder areas. Glossy green 2" leaves. Small creamy flowers are billowy mass late spring through fall. May be cut to ground in winter to control.

V13
Trumpet
Honey-
suckle

V14
Cat's Claw

V15
Mattress
Vine

V16
Boston Ivy

V17
Passion
Vine

V18
Silver
Lace Vine

Vines

	Important Characteristics					Cultural Preferences			Tolerances									Aesthetic and Cultural Compatibility
Plant name and description	Deciduous	Evergreen	Flowers	Fall Color	Fruit	Growth Rate	Full Sun	Part Shade	Well Drained Soil	Monthly Irrigation	No Water After 2nd Yr.	Alkaline Soil	Seacoast Conditions	Sprinklers	Wind	Heat	Sunset Zones	

V19 Rosa banksiae—Lady Banks Rose

Two evergreen, spineless roses. Small, medium green divided foliage is glossy and resistant to almost all insects and diseases. *R.b. 'Lutea'*, a shrubby plant, double 2" yellow roses, *R.b. 'Alba Plena'* with 6" clusters of semi-double fragrant white flowers.

Evergreen ●, Flowers ●; Growth Rate F; Full Sun ●; Well Drained Soil ●, Monthly Irrigation ●; Sprinklers ●; Wind ●, Heat ● ●; Sunset Zones 4-24. T56,65 TS14,16 GC13,16,17,29 P11 B7

V20 Rosa 'Cecile Brunner'—Cecile Brunner Rose

Can be a large shrub or a climber. Typical divided rose foliage, but free of most insects. Light pink, 2" double flowers are borne in 6" to 8" clusters in spring and summer. Individual buds are 1" perfect boutonnieres.

Deciduous ●, Flowers ●; Growth Rate F; Full Sun ●; Monthly Irrigation ●; Sprinklers ●; Wind ●, Heat ● ●; Sunset Zones 4-24. T52,56 TS16,50,56 SS5 P20 B2

V21 Solanum jasminoides—Potato Vine

An extremely fast growth habit and almost perpetual bloom make this an excellent arbor cover. Semideciduous in colder areas. White 1" flowers are borne in clusters of 8 to 12.

Deciduous ●, Flowers ● ●; Growth Rate VF; Full Sun ●; Sprinklers ●; Wind ●, Heat ●; Sunset Zones 8,9 12-24. T15,39 TS9,11 SS5 GC19 P4,16 B11

V22 Thunbergia alata—Black-Eyed Susan

A perennial vine often grown as a summer blooming annual. May not regrow after a 22° frost or if roots are overwet during winter. 3" triangular leaves cover the long vines; 1" tubular bright orange flowers with a dark brown throat are scattered over the vines in summer.

Deciduous ●, Flowers ●; Growth Rate F; Full Sun ●; Part Shade ●, Well Drained Soil ●; Sprinklers ●; Heat ●; Sunset Zones ALL. T11 TS47,49 S13 V3,15 GC30,31 P2,11 AB13

V23 Vitis vinifera—Grape

Very fast growth makes this a good arbor cover but requires heavy pruning every winter; 4" to 8" maple-like leaves may be dark green on top, white or green beneath, borne on heavy canes. If fruit is desired, choose varieties best suited to your climate.

Deciduous ●, Fruit ●; Growth Rate VF; Full Sun ●; Monthly Irrigation ●; Alkaline Soil ●; Wind ●, Heat ●; Sunset Zones ALL. T2,39 TS40,59 GC3,19 P46,48,60 B2

V24 Wisteria species—Wisteria

Fast growing to 40'. Lavender, blue, white, or pink flowers in 12" to 24" long pendulous clusters April to May. May not bloom for several years after planting. Annual pruning recommended. Grafted forms offer predictable flower colors, seed grown plants do not.

Deciduous ●, Flowers ●; Growth Rate M-F; Full Sun ●, Part Shade ●; Well Drained Soil ●; Heat ●; Sunset Zones ALL. T51,52,62 TS51,58 GC4,8 P16 AB7

V19
Lady Banks
Rose

V20
Cecile
Brunner
Rose

V21
Potato Vine

V22
Black-Eyed
Susan

V23
Grape

V24
Wisteria

82

Ornamental Grasses

	Important Characteristics				Cultural Preferences				Tolerances								Aesthetic and Cultural Compatibility
Plant name and description	Evergreen Deciduous	Flowers	Fall Color	Fruit	Growth Rate	Full Sun	Part Shade	Well Drained Soil	Monthly Irrigation	No Water After 2nd Yr.	Alkaline Soil	Seacoast Conditions	Sprinklers	Wind	Heat	Sunset Zones	
OG1 CN *Festuca californica*—California Fescue		●	●		M	●		●	●	●		●		●	●	● ALL	T53-56 TS47,54 SS5 V2 GC23 P23 AB2,3 B3,7
OG2 *Helictotrichon sempervirens*—Blue Oat Grass	●		●		M	●			●		●		●	●	●	● ALL	T39,42 TS2,54 SS2 GC23,24 P12,23 AB15 B2
OG3 *Miscanthus sinensis zebrinus*—Zebra Grass	●	●	●		F	●							●	●		● ALL	T11,40 TS54,66,68 SS7,8 GC20,30 P17,24 AB12 B4
OG4 CN *Muehlenbergia rigens*—Deer Grass	●		●		M	●		●	●	●			●		●	● ALL	T42 TS8,54 SS1 GC16,29 P18 AB1,5 B8
OG5 *Pennisetum alopecuroides*—Fountain Grass	●			●	M	●		●		●		●		●	●	● ALL	T20,33 TS54 SS6,14 GC32,34 P45,47 AB3,4,11 B4
OG6 CN *Stipa pulchra*—Needle Grass	●		●		M	●	●		●						●	● ALL	T6,9 TS54,78 SS16 V19 GC33 P37,58 AB9,10,12 B9,12

OG1 CN *Festuca californica*—California Fescue

Fine-leafed bunch grass grows 3-4' tall, nearly as broad. Color ranges from grassy green to blue gray. Remains green through the summer, is a tougher plant than its appearance indicates. Does well from seed, division or planted out from containers. Excellent in natural areas. Much more drought tolerant than *F. ovina glauca*, especially inland.

OG2 *Helictotrichon sempervirens*—Blue Oat Grass

Silvery blue-gray with a fine fountain-like structure resembling blue fescue *(Festuca ovina glauca)* only larger, 2-3'. Useful massed or used singly as accent. Likes good drainage, does best in sun or part shade—will take more shade if watered less. Combines well with other grasses and broadleafed plants; good in rock gardens.

OG3 *Miscanthus sinensis zebrinus*—Zebra Grass

A large and tall clumping grass growing 5-7' high and almost as wide, with medium green color and yellow bands. The yellow striping fades in too much shade, and plants do not produce as much variegation when young. Good for big borders and as seasonal accent. It dies down in winter. Needs to be eased into drought tolerance from lush containers.

OG4 CN *Muehlenbergia rigens*—Deer Grass

Large bunch with stiff, fine green leaves and gray-green flower spikes. Attains a full, broad habit in loamy soil, but is slower where planted in clay soils. Mature clumps are about 3-4', equally wide, very hemispherical. Lovely in natural areas where movement of the flower stalks adds interest. Sometimes gray flowers are cut to better view green foliage.

OG5 *Pennisetum alopecuroides*—Fountain Grass

The species from which many of the Fountain Grass varieties have been derived. Grows 3-4' high with a light green foliage turning yellow in fall, then rich brown in winter. Flowers are pinkish, slightly nodding and good cut. Preferred over *P. setaceum* since it doesn't seed invasively. Varieties *P. caudatum*—white flower, *P. orientale*—pink flower.

OG6 CN *Stipa pulchra*—Needle Grass

Probably most versatile bunch grass for natural areas of landscaping at garden edges, hillsides, etc. Grows in many wild, natural areas in CA. Thrives in full sun, clay soil and with little water, providing a 2-4' cover. Sets seed by May, then dries to a pale gold. Can be cut to remove the dry stalks. Because of sharp awns on seeds, it shouldn't be grazed after flowering. Naturalizes in 3-4 yrs.

OG1
California
Fescue

OG2
Blue Oat
Grass

OG3
Zebra
Grass

OG4
Deer Grass

OG5
Fountain
Grass

OG6
Needle
Grass

84

Groundcovers

		Important Characteristics					Cultural Preferences				Tolerances								
	Plant name and description	Deciduous	Evergreen	Flowers	Fall Color	Fruit	Growth Rate	Full Sun	Part Shade	Well Drained Soil	Monthly Irrigation	No Water After 2nd Yr.	Alkaline Soil	Seacoast Conditions	Sprinklers	Wind	Heat	Sunset Zones	Aesthetic and Cultural Compatibility
GC1	***Acacia redolens***		•	•			VF	•				•		•	•	•	• •	12-24	T7,18 TS11,12,14-16,24,25,29 P2,28 B1,2
GC2	***Achillea tomentosa*—Woolly Yarrow**		•	•			M	•	•	•	•				•	•		ALL	P2,26,54
GC3	***Armeria maritima*—Sea Thrift**		•	•			S	•		•	•			•	•	•	•	ALL	T20 GC1,23,24 P34
GC4 CN	***Arctostaphylos hookeri*—Monterey Manzanita**		•	•			S-M	•	•	•	•			•		•	•	6-9 14-17	T41-43,45, 53,62 TS4-7,21 SS14 GC30 P42
GC5 CN	***Artostaphylos 'Point Reyes'*—Pt. Reyes Manzanita**		•	•			F	•	•	•				•	•	•		1-9 14-17	T25,53,62 TS3,16 SS1,5 GC9 P29,43 B2,7
GC6 CN	***Baccharis pilularis 'Twin Peaks', 'Pigeon Point'*— Dwarf Coyote Brush**		•				VF	•		•				•	•	•	•	5-11 14-24	T7,15,16 TS11,12,14, 23,31 GC1,17,29 P37,43 B2,7

GC1 ***Acacia redolens***

This prostrate Acacia will reach 2' to 2-1/2' tall, 25' spread in two to three years. The narrow 3" long leaves are gray-green. Flowers are 1/2" yellow balls blooming for 4 to 6 weeks in spring. Good under Blue Gums and in serpentine soil. Short lived with frequent irrigation.

GC2 ***Achillea tomentosa*—Woolly Yarrow**

This perennial develops into a spreading mat of hairy, green fern-like leaves. Golden yellow flowers in flat clusters on 6" stems. Excellent between stepping stones. Must have good drainage.

GC3 ***Armeria maritima*—Sea Thrift**

Tufted 1' wide mounds of grasslike foliage to 8" tall. Rose pink 1" ball-like clusters of flowers on stalks above foliage appear in masses in spring in zones 14, 15, 16, all year in zone 17. Shear to remove old flowers.

GC4 CN ***Arctostaphylos hookeri*—Monterey Manzanita**

Best in sandy soil under pines, but tolerates some clay. *A.h. 'Wayside'* forms 2-1/2' tall "billowy" habit. *A.h. 'Monterey Carpet'* will reach 1' by 4' to 6' spread. Best in north or east or part shade exposures in zones 14 and 15. White flowers in spring.

GC5 CN ***Artostaphylos 'Point Reyes'*—Pt. Reyes Manzanita**

Prostrate, spreading 15'. Dependable flowering. Spatulate 3/4" dark green leaves tolerate smog. Needs some water to fill in. Best on east or north exposure slopes with an annual fertilizer application and drip irrigation.

GC6 CN ***Baccharis pilularis 'Twin Peaks', 'Pigeon Point'*—Dwarf Coyote Brush**

Both male forms provide a uniform cover 8" to 24" high with 6' spread. A dense mound to 2' with time. Bright green 1/2" foliage looks better with monthly watering. Shear annually from first year to keep low. Treat for Lacebug if bleached foliage is found.

GC1
Acacia
redolens

GC2
Woolly
Yarrow

GC3
Sea Thrift

GC4
Monterey
Manzanita

GC5
Point Reyes
Manzanita

GC6
Dwarf
Coyote
Brush

Plant name and description	Dec.	Evgn.	Flwrs	Fall Color	Fruit	Growth Rate	Full Sun	Part Shade	Well Drained Soil	Monthly Irrigation	No Water After 2nd Yr.	Alkaline Soil	Seacoast Cond.	Sprinklers	Wind	Heat	Sunset Zones	Aesthetic and Cultural Compatibility
GC7 *Bergenia crassifolia*—Winter Blooming Bergenia — Dark green 8" diameter oval leaves lay flat, all facing up. A bold textured 12" high groundcover best in part shade. Winter blooming pink or bright rose flowers in clusters stand on 12" stalks.		●	●			S		●				●	●	●		●	1-9 14-24	T4,61 TS60 SS11,14 GC36 P1,8,30,39 AB13 B11
GC8 CN *Ceanothus gloriosus porrectus*—Mount Vision Ceanothus — Usually under 2' tall but 6' to 8' broad. Small, dark green spiny leaves contrast with lavender-blue flowers in spring. One of the toughest prostrate ceanothus.		●	●			M-F	●	●	●	●					●	●	4-7 14-24	T16,53-56, 58 TS4,9,11,12, 14,69 GC9,11,15 P46,57
GC9 CN *Ceanothus hearstiorum*—Hearst Ceanothus — To 3" tall, 6' to 8' spread. Dark green, glossy 1" leaves are covered with glands. Use only on north or east slopes in zones 14, 15, any exposure zone 17. Medium blue flowers in spring. A dense mat at its best. Drip watering only.		●	●			F	●		●	●				●	●	●	14-24	T53,62 TS4,5,11,14, 22 SS2 GC1,15,19 AB3,10 P55,57,60
GC10 CN *Ceanothus maritimus* — Gray-green 3/4" angular foliage covers the 12-18" tall, 6' wide scrambling groundcover. Medium blue florets in dense 1" clusters are scattered through the foliage in spring. Do not use sprinklers.		●	●			M	●					●		●			14-17	T2,5 TS25,35 SS6 GC1,11 P40,42
GC11 CN *Ceanothus rigidus* 'Snowball' — Mounding shrub usually 3' tall, 6' to 8' broad. The 3/4" spiny foliage is hidden in spring when white flowers cover the plant. The most drought tolerant ceanothus available. Long lived.		●	●	●		M	●	●				●			●	●	4-7 14-24	T2,20 TS31,33 SS6 GC29 P19 AB10
GC12 *Cerastium tomentosum*—Snow-in-Summer — Silver gray 3/4" leaves thickly cover the 4" thick mat. 1/2" pure white flowers may completely cover the plants in June-July. Only for well-drained soil. Fertilize 3 times per year.		●	●			M	●	●	●					●	●		ALL	T8,9,24 TS24 SS18 V9 GC13 P12,32 AB12 B1,6

GC7
Winter
Blooming
Bergenia

GC8
Mount
Vision
Ceanothus

GC9
Hearst
Ceanothus

GC10
Ceanothus
maritimus

GC11
Snowball
Ceanothus

GC12
Snow-in-
Summer

88

Groundcovers

Plant name and description	Deciduous	Evergreen	Flowers	Fall Color	Fruit	Growth Rate	Full Sun	Part Shade	Well Drained Soil	Monthly Irrigation	No Water After 2nd Yr.	Alkaline Soil	Seacoast Conditions	Sprinklers	Wind	Heat	Sunset Zones	Aesthetic and Cultural Compatibility
GC13 *Ceratostigma plumbaginoides*—Dwarf Plumbago		●	●		●	M-F	●	●	●	●	●					●	14-24	P8,28,36,38 AB7,13
GC14 *Chamaemelum nobile*—Chamomile			●			F	●	●	●					●			ALL	T14,23 TS1,6 SS1,13 V3 OG1,4,5 GC2 P7,31 AB2,13 B3,6,7
GC15 *Cistus salvifolius*—Sageleaf Rockrose		●	●			F	●						●		●	●	7-9 12-15 18-22 best, 16,17 23,24	T4,42,43 TS32 GC6,34 P4,34,60 AB10
GC16 *Coprosma kirkii*—Creeping Coprosma		●				M	●		●		●		●	●	●	●	8,9 14-17 21-24	T12,16 TS12,14,15,58,60 GC6,17 P57,59 AB2
GC17 *Coprosma pumila* 'Verde Vista'		●				S-M	●		●		●		●	●	●	●	8,9 14-17 21-24	T16,60 TS1,18,26 GC4,5 P26
GC18 *Epimedium grandiflorum* 'Rose Queen'—Bishop's Hat		●	●			S		●		●					●	●	1-9 14-17	T2,52 TS44,49 SS14,15 OG1,4 GC28 P1,20,29,30 B3,5

GC13 *Ceratostigma plumbaginoides*—Dwarf Plumbago

A wiry-stemmed groundcover to 6" to 12" tall. Leaves are bronze-green in heat, drought or cold, dark green in shade with winter. Fluorescent blue 1/2" flowers from summer to October or November. Can form large mats. Semi-evergreen. Will tolerate watering or drought.

GC14 *Chamaemelum nobile*—Chamomile

A soft, cushion-like 3" high bright green cover is formed in two years if divisions are planted 12" apart in March. The fragrant foliage will fill between stepping stones, topped by yellow button-like flowers appearing in spring. Excellent dry-shade groundcover.

GC15 *Cistus salvifolius*—Sageleaf Rockrose

Spreading habit to 2' by 6'. Gray-green leaves. White 1" flowers with yellow spots in late spring. Growth habit is like a low growing White Rockrose.

GC16 *Coprosma kirkii*—Creeping Coprosma

Spreading shrub 2' to 3' tall. Olive green 1/2" foliage. Shear in spring to keep 1' high, then fertilize. A tough, utilitarian ground cover.

GC17 *Coprosma pumila* 'Verde Vista'

Mounding cover to 2-1/2' tall with an 8' spread. Glossy, yellow-green 1/2" leaves densely cover the mound-shaped plant. Extremely drought tolerant. No fruit produced.

GC18 *Epimedium grandiflorum* 'Rose Queen'—Bishop's Hat

Light green, divided evergreen leaves are mindful of their relative Nandina. Leaflets up to 3" long are bronze-pink in spring, bronze in fall. Twelve inch spikes of red or yellow small flowers appear in spring. Excellent dry-shade ground cover.

GC13
Dwarf
Plumbago

GC14
Chamo-
mile

GC15
Sageleaf
Rockrose

GC16
Creeping
Coprosma

GC17
Verde Vista
Coprosma

GC18
Bishop's
Hat

Groundcovers

Plant name and description	Deciduous	Evergreen	Flowers	Fall Color	Fruit	Growth Rate	Full Sun	Part Shade	Well Drained Soil	Monthly Irrigation	No Water After 2nd Yr.	Alkaline Soil	Seacoast Conditions	Sprinklers	Wind	Heat	Sunset Zones	Aesthetic and Cultural Compatibility
GC19 *Gazania* species and hybrids — Clumping green or gray-green foliage to 6" tall with orange, maroon or yellow 2" to 3" daisies, or trailing gray or gray-green foliage with yellow flowers. Hybrids between these, as *Mitsuwa Yellow* seem the most tolerant of poorly drained soils.		●	●			M-F	●		●	●	●		●	●	●	●	8-24	T4,17 TS21 GC1,6 P1,2,4,5,28 AB1
GC20 *Hypericum calycinum*—St. John's Wort — A hardy ground cover which can be invasive. The 2" dull green leaves cover the 1' tall stiff stems forming a full cover of foliage. 2" yellow flowers appear in early summer and bloom intermittently through the year. Mow to 3" tall in March and fertilize.		●	●			F	●		●		●	●		●	●	●	4-24	T18 do not plant with low shrubs
GC21 Ice Plant — *Delosperma alba*—White Trailing Ice Plant: Good bank cover, white flowers not showy.		●	●			F	●		●		●	●	●	●	●	●	12-24	T39,57 P42,43 B11
Drosanthemum floribundum—Rosea Ice Plant: Good erosion control, 6" tall, covered with pale pink flowers late spring, early summer.		●	●			F	●		●		●	●	●	●	●	●	12-24	
GC22 Ice Plant — Most of the blindingly bright Ice Plant seen is one of these: *Lampranthus aurantiacus*—Yellow flowers February to May.		●	●			F	●		●		●	●	●	●	●	●	12-24	TS24,25,50,63,64
Lampranthus spectabilis—Pink, rose, red, purple, 12" tall.		●	●			F	●		●		●	●	●	●	●	●	12-24	
Malephora crocea—Reddish yellow flowers, 6" high sparsely produced through the year.		●	●			F	●		●		●	●	●	●	●	●	12-24	
GC23 *Juniperus chinensis* 'Parsonii'—Prostrata Juniper — Flat, heavy branches trail along the ground forming a cover 1' to 2' high by 10' wide. Gray-green spiny foliage. Water mold tolerant. An excellent barrier plant.		●				F	●		●				●		●	●	ALL	T11,39 TS50,59 SS14 GC19 P20,26
GC24 *Juniperus virginiana* 'Silver Spreader' — To 18" tall, 8' spread. A full cover of bright silver-gray foliage. Fast growing, easy, more resistant to root fungus problems than most Junipers.		●				F	●		●		●		●		●	●	ALL	T13,20 TS50,59,68 SS14 P20

GC19
Gazania

GC20
St. John's
Wort

GC21
Ice Plant

GC22
Ice Plant

GC23
Prostrata
Juniper

GC24
Silver
Spreader
Juniper

Groundcovers

	Important Characteristics					Cultural Preferences			Tolerances									Aesthetic and Cultural Compatibility
Plant name and description	Deciduous	Evergreen	Flowers	Fall Color	Fruit	Growth Rate	Full Sun	Part Shade	Well Drained Soil	Monthly Irrigation	No Water After 2nd Yr	Alkaline Soil	Seacoast Conditions	Sprinklers	Wind	Heat	Sunset Zones	
GC25 *Oenothera berlandierii*—Mexican Evening Primrose	•	•				VF	•				•			•	•	•	ALL	TS50 P41,55 AB3
GC26 *Phyla nodiflora*—Lippia	•	•				F	•						•	•	•	•	8-24	T41,56 TS61,65 SS6,9 V18 OG3 GC6,31 P2,24 AB6,12,14 B1,2
GC27 *Polygonum capitatum*—Pink Knotweed	•	•	•	•		F	•	•	•	•		•		•	•	•	8-9 12-24	T40,58 TS67,78 SS1,3 V17 OG5 GC6 P44,47 AB1 B4
GC28 CN *Ribes viburnifolium*—Evergreen Currant		•				M	•	•	•					•			8,9 14-24	T53,55,56,62 TS2,3,46,66 SS14 P20,29
GC29 *Rosemarinus officinalis cultivars*—Rosemary		•	•			F	•		•		•		•	•	•	•	4-24	T39,41,52 TS11,12,14,22 GC1,24,31 AB3
GC30 *Scaevola 'Mauve Clusters'*—Fan Flower		•	•			F	•	•	•	•			•	•	•	•	14-17	T14 TS11,59 GC1,2,4,6 AB13

GC25 *Oenothera berlandierii*—Mexican Evening Primrose

A spectacular display of light pink 1-1/2" flowers most of the summer if mowed to 3", fertilized and watered June 1 and August 15. The upright stems hold the flowers 8" to 12" high. Can be invasive if overwatered. May be deciduous for 45 days in winter.

GC26 *Phyla nodiflora*—Lippia

A flat mat of 3/4" green leaves hug the ground forming a drought tolerant lawn substitute. The 1/2" verbena-like flowers attract many bees. Mow to 1" tall to remove them. Tolerates full, hot sun to part shade. May go deciduous in winter without fertilizer.

GC27 *Polygonum capitatum*—Pink Knotweed

The 1-1/2" leaves are dark green turning pink as they mature. Evergreen unless temperatures go below 28°F. A spreading groundcover to 6-8" tall, the dark pink leaves contrast with the light pink small flowers. A quick, tough groundcover for any soil.

GC28 CN *Ribes viburnifolium*—Evergreen Currant

Arching open habit, 3' high, spreading 12'. Shiny, dark green aromatic 1-1/2" round foliage on wine red stems. Inconspicuous flowers. Small red berries. Grow in part shade. Excellent under old oaks. Prune to 12" in spring to keep dense.

GC29 *Rosemarinus officinalis cultivars*—Rosemary

Narrow 1" green leaves with pungent fragrance, and grayish undersides. *R.o. prostrata* has medium green foliage and pale blue flowers. Best spilling over a wall. *R.o. 'Collingwood Ingram'* to 2-1/2" tall, dark green foliage, brilliant blue flowers. Good border.

GC30 *Scaevola 'Mauve Clusters'*—Fan Flower

A bright green low mound or mat of 1" toothed leaves like a Dwarf Coyote Brush with flowers. It may be almost covered with 1/2" lavender fan-shaped flowers in spring, but will continue to bear some until October. May be frost damaged in zones 14-15.

GC25
Mexican
Evening
Primrose

GC26
Lippia

GC27
Pink
Knotweed

GC28
Evergreen
Currant

GC29
Rosemary

GC30
Fan
Flower

94

Groundcovers

Plant name and description	Deciduous	Evergreen	Flowers	Fall Color	Fruit	Growth Rate	Well Drained Soil	Part Shade	Full Sun	No Water After 2nd Yr	Monthly Irrigation	Alkaline Soil	Seacoast Conditions	Sprinklers	Wind	Heat	Sunset Zones	Aesthetic and Cultural Compatibility
GC31 Stachys byzantina—Lamb's Ears White, woolly 3" leaves lay flat on the prostrate stems. These form circular clumps to 6" high and 2' spread. Small lavender flowers are buried in the white wool of the 18" tall flower stems appearing in June.			•	•		S	•	•	•	•			•	•	•	•	ALL	T2 TS40 GC5 P28,34,36
GC32 Teucrium chamaedrys—Germander Toothed dark green 3/4" leaves form on upright stems to 1' tall. Planted from bands 4" to 6" apart, forms a neat informal or sheared hedge. Reddish-purple flowers are scattered over them in summer.			•	•		M	•	•	•	•					•	•	ALL	T11 TS6,7,62 P26,55
GC33 Thymus sp.—Thyme Ranging between 1" tall groundcovers for use between stepping stones or as small area fragrant groundcovers, as *T. herba-barona*. Up to 12" tall shrubs as *T. citriodorus*. All useful for flavoring foods.			•	•		S	•		•	•				•	•	•	ALL	T46,48 TS76,77 SS2,5 V9,12 OG6 GC13,15 P57,58 AB3,13 B5,8,9
GC34 Verbena tenuisecta—Moss Verbena A perennial verbena hardy to 15°F. Dark green, finely cut foliage on a densely covered mounded groundcover. Brilliant lavender flowers cover the plant beginning in April. Mow to 3" in May and August and fertilize to maintain a neat, even planting.			•	•		F.	•		•		•	•	•		•	•	14-17	T4 TS29 AB3
GC35 Viola labradorica A beautifully invasive groundcover for semi-shade. Maroon 1-1/2" kidney-shaped leaves contrast with the 1/2" lavender-blue flowers. Reseeds and spreads by runners.			•	•		F		•		•		•			•	•	ALL	T10,13 TS1,30 SS4,14 V4,5 OG5 GC7,36 P6,8 AB13,18 B1,12
GC36 Viola odorata—Sweet Violet Dark green 4" heart-shaped leaves form 6" high clumps. Intensely fragrant flowers of purple, lavender, pink or white are borne above the foliage in spring. Best in part to deep shade. Mow off old foliage in December to February. Can be very invasive.			•	•		M		•		•		•		•	•	•	ALL	T17,52-55 TS3,21 SS11 V10 GC28,35 P1,8 AB18 B7,11

GC31
Lamb's
Ears

GC32
Germander

GC33
Thyme

GC34
Moss
Verbena

GC35
Viola
labradorica

GC36
Sweet
Violet

96

Perennials

Plant name and description	Important Characteristics					Cultural Preferences			Tolerances									
	Deciduous	Evergreen	Flowers	Fall Color	Fruit	Growth Rate	Full Sun	Part Shade	Well Drained Soil	Monthly Irrigation	No Water After 2nd Yr	Seacoast Conditions	Alkaline Soil	Sprinklers	Wind	Heat	Sunset Zones	Aesthetic and Cultural Compatibility
P1 *Acanthus mollis*—Bear's Breech		•	•	•		F	•			•		•	•	•	•	•	4-24	TS49 SS14 GC13 P4,5,29
P2 *Achillea filipendulina*—Fernleaf Yarrow		•	•			M	•		•	•	•		•		•	•	ALL	T10 TS11,12 GC2 P11,34
P3 *Achillea millefolium*—Common Yarrow, Milfoil		•	•			F	•		•	•	•	•	•		•	•	ALL	T53,55 GC2 P6
P4 *Agapanthus africanus, Agapanthus orientalis*—Lily-of-the-Nile			•	•		F	•	•		•		•		•	•	•	7-9 12-24	T2,25,45 TS20,50,58,59 SS5,6 GC9,23,24,30 B2,8,11
P5 *Aloe species*—Aloe			•	•		M	•	•	•			•		•	•	•	8,9 12-24	T39,60 TS17-19,24,25,29 SS6,7,8 GC19 P1,25
P6 *Arctotis Hybrids*—African Daisy			•	•		M	•		•		•	•	•	•	•	•	7-9 14-24	SS7,8,18 P3,34

P1 — Acanthus mollis—Bear's Breech
Basal leaves to 2' wide on broomsticklike leaf stems are dark shining green. They are held 3' high forming a 6' wide dome. White, spiny flowers are held on 4' tall spikes in spring. Will go dormant in summer in an unwatered site. Full or partial shade.

P2 — Achillea filipendulina—Fernleaf Yarrow
Fernlike leaves clothe the base of the 3' to 4' tall stems, on top of which are 4" to 6" broad, flat dense heads of bright yellow flowers in early summer. Excellent for dried or fresh flower arrangements.

P3 — Achillea millefolium—Common Yarrow, Milfoil
Narrow fernlike, gray-green leaves form a clump to 2'. Stiff 3' tall stems bear 2-1/2" to 3" flat clusters of white flowers through summer. Can be mowed to 3" tall. *A.m. rosea* has rose-colored flowers; *'Fire King'* has dark rose flowers fading to light pink.

P4 — Agapanthus africanus, Agapanthus orientalis—Lily-of-the-Nile
Clumps of 12", straplike leaves support rigid, 18" stalks of 20-100 blue or white flowers in June to fall. Tolerates drought after establishment but looks better with water. A dwarf white is sometimes available. *'Peter Pan'* is a dwarf form.

P5 — Aloe species—Aloe
All species are rosettes of fleshy, pointed leaves which form clumps from 8" to 18" tall. Tubular flowers held in clusters on stalks above the foliage can be yellow, orange, or pink. Full sun near the coast or in part shade under old oaks. Good border.

P6 — Arctotis Hybrids—African Daisy
Gray-green divided, coarse foliage makes a mound 8" to 12" tall, 3' spread. Daisylike 3" flowers by dozens appear on 8" stalks above the foliage in spring, and sporadically through the summer, if spent flowers are removed. Colors in white, red, orange, yellow or purple with a black eye.

P1
Bear's
Breech

P2
Fernleaf
Yarrow

P3
Common
Yarrow

P4
Lily-of-the-
Nile

P5
Aloe

P6
African
Daisy

98

Perennials

Plant name and description	Important Characteristics					Cultural Preferences			Tolerances									Aesthetic and Cultural Compatibility
	Deciduous	Evergreen	Flowers	Fall Color	Fruit	Growth Rate	Full Sun	Part Shade	Well Drained Soil	Monthly Irrigation	No Water After 2nd Yr	Alkaline Soil	Seacoast Conditions	Sprinklers	Wind	Heat	Sunset Zones	
P7 *Artemisia schmidtiana 'Silver Mound'*—Angel's Hair		●				F	●	●			●				●	●	ALL	TS11 SS18 P22,34 AB13
P8 *Aspidistra elatoir*—Cast Iron Plant		●				S		●		●		●	●	●	●	●	12-24	TS49,72 SS14 F all
P9 *Aster frikartii 'Wonder of Stafa', 'Monch'*		●	●			F	●					●			●	●	ALL	T61,64 TS8,29 SS2,17 V18,20 OG5 GC2,13,32 P4,10 AB2,13 B2,12
P10 *Aubrieta deltoides*—Common Aubrieta		●	●			M	●	●	●								1-9 14-21	T1,33 TS2,8,28 SS2,7,8 V19 GC2,15,30 P33
P11 *Aurinia saxatilis*—Perennial Alyssum		●	●			S-M	●		●	●					●	●	ALL	T10,23 GC9 P3
P12 *Calocephalus brownii*—Cushion Bush		●				M	●		●			●			●	●	16-19	T39,45 TS11,20 SS10,18 V8,21 OG2 GC13,30,31 P10,14 B5

P7 *Artemisia schmidtiana 'Silver Mound'*—Angel's Hair

A woody perennial growing into dense, silvery-white 8" tall mound. Insignificant flowers. Must have good drainage. Excellent creeping over rocks. Will not tolerate sprinklers.

P8 *Aspidistra elatoir*—Cast Iron Plant

The tropical looking 2' long, dark green leaves emerge from the ground to form a clump which can gradually enlarge in diameter. Will grow in very dark places but sunburns in direct sun. Very long lived in any soil. Check for Spider Mites in summer.

P9 *Aster frikartii 'Wonder of Stafa', 'Monch'*

Among the most useful of perennials. *A. frikartii* dependably produces large quantities of blue-lavender 2-1/2" daisies above the 2' tall stems 12 months per year if spent flowers are removed regularly.

P10 *Aubrieta deltoides*—Common Aubrieta

A 3' tall, 18" circle of small, toothed soft gray-green leaves. One-half inch lilac, purple or white flowers are dotted over the plant in early to late spring. Use in full sun in zones 16, 17, filtered shade in 14,15. Prune off spent flowers but not much foliage.

P11 *Aurinia saxatilis*—Perennial Alyssum

A perennial cluster of 2" long, gray-green foliage, 8" to 12" tall. Dense cover of golden yellow flowers in spring. Shear off old flowers after blooming and fertilize. *A.s. compacta* is 6", tight form.

P12 *Calocephalus brownii*—Cushion Bush

A silver-white 3' cushion of thread-like twigs. The dense rounded form is topped with 1/2" button-shaped white flowers in late spring. Best on the coast (zone 17) but successful in 16. May be frost killed at 26 degrees. Must have well drained soil.

P7
Angel's
Hair

P8
Cast Iron
Plant

P9
Aster
frikartii

P10
Common
Aubrieta

P11
Perennial
Alyssum

P12
Cushion
Bush

100

Plant name and description

P13 Campanula portenschlagiana (C. murialis)—Dalmatian Bell Flower

A 4" high mat of heart-shaped 1-1/2" deep green toothed leaves are beautiful year round. When smothered by 1" bell-shaped, brilliant violet-blue flowers from April to June drifts of this Campanula are the star of the garden. They may bloom again during August or fall if old flowers are removed.

P14 Centaurea cineraria—Dusty Miller

Silver-white, deeply cut foliage covers the shrubby 18" tall plant. Cut the yellow or purple flowers off to maintain the plant vigor. Tip prune frequently to keep them bushy.

P15 Centranthus ruber—Jupiter's Beard

This is the roadside volunteer which produces 6-8" clusters of light pink, rose pink or white 1/4" flowers all summer. Each 18" - 24" stem has 8-10 3" long green leaves, topped by a flower cluster. The 3-4" deep carrot-like root makes this plant extremely drought tolerant and difficult to eradicate if planted in the wrong place.

P16 Chrysanthemum frutescens—Marguerite

A 3' to 5' woody perennial ball of green or gray lacy foliage. Green foliage forms bear yellow, white, pink, or multicolored single or double daisies. 'Silver Princess' to 3', gray foliage. Shear to remove flowers in July, September. Replace every two to three years.

P17 Chrysanthemum parthenium—Feverfew

The 18" tall vertical stems are fully covered by yellow-green 1" leaves which have a strong odor. This form can reseed aggressively from the 1" white daisy-like flowers. 'Golden Ball' has yellow ball-like flowers and does not reseed. 'Aureum' has chartreuse foliage.

P18 Coreopsis auriculata 'Nana'—Tickseed

This 3-4" high mat of 2-1/2" dark green leaves produces quantities of 2" orange daisies on 6" stems all summer. It performs best with a thorough watering every two weeks. May lose foliage below 22°F.

	Important Characteristics					Cultural Preferences			Tolerances								Sunset Zones	Aesthetic and Cultural Compatibility
	Deciduous	Evergreen	Flowers	Fall Color	Fruit	Growth Rate	Full Sun	Part Shade	Well Drained Soil	Monthly Irrigation	No Water After 2nd Yr.	Alkaline Soil	Seacoast Conditions	Sprinklers	Wind	Heat		
P13		●	●			M	●	●	●							●	14-24	T52,61 TS44,70,72 SS11,13 V4,7 OG1 GC31 P22,27 AB13 B12
P14		●	●			M	●			●	●			●	●	●	8-24	TS17-19 GC34 P42,60
P15		●	●			S	●			●	●		●	●	●	●	15-24	T1,9 TS2,12 SS7,8,18 V14 OG5 GC1,25 P1,5 AB1,5 B2,10
P16		●	●			F	●			●			●		●	●	any above 18°F	TS50,58 P22,43
P17			●			F	●						●	●		●	ALL	T2,26 TS30,65 SS1,16 V23 OG3 GC2,31 P14,18 AB6,8 B6,7
P18		●	●			S	●	●	●	●			●	●	●	●	15-24	T39,44 TS3,11,37 SS1,5 GC26,31 AB2,6

P13
Dalmatian
Bell Flower

P14
Dusty
Miller

P15
Jupiter's
Beard

P16
Marguerite

P17
Feverfew

P18
Tickseed

102

Perennials

Plant name and description	Important Characteristics					Cultural Preferences				Tolerances								Sunset Zones	Aesthetic and Cultural Compatibility
	Deciduous	Evergreen	Flowers	Fall Color	Fruit	Growth Rate	Full Sun	Part Shade	Well Drained Soil	Monthly Irrigation	No Water After 2nd Yr.	Alkaline Soil	Seacoast Conditions	Sprinklers	Wind	Heat			
P19 CN *Diplacus hybrids*—Monkey Flower. Shrubby perennials to 2-1/2' tall, 4' spread. Verity hybrids have 1-1/2" tubular flowers of white, buff, rose, orange, maroon, and 1" dark, glossy green foliage. Flowers begin in April through June. Prune to 1-1/2' to 2' after flowering and water and they begin flowering again.			•	•		F	•	•		•				•	•	•		14-24	T15 TS11,12 SS2 GC8,9,11,15,30 P46,48
P20 *Dietes vegeta*—Fortnight Lily. Narrow, swordlike 2' to 4' tall leaves. Flowers are 3" wide waxy white miniatures of Japanese Iris with orange and brown blotches in the center. The same flower stems produce flowers for many years.			•	•		M	•	•		•		•	•	•	•	•		13-24	T9 SS14 GC34 P29,59
P21 *Erigeron karvinskianus*—Fleabane. A tangled pile of twigs 10" to 20" tall, thinly covered by 1" toothed leaves; 3/4" white daisies are sprinkled over the plant most of the year. May be sheared to any form, including as a groundcover; or used in hanging baskets. 'Mariesii' has 1" pink flowers in profusion.			•	•		F	•	•				•	•	•	•	•		12-24	T14,19 TS4,5,17-19,53 SS18 GC32 P46-48,56 B7
P22 *Erysimum hieraciifolium*—Siberian Wallflower. Selected forms from 18" tall to flat mats, all have 2" long medium green leaves. Clusters of 1-1/2", rich orange fragrant flowers appear for 30 days in spring. 'Jubilee Gold' is a long blooming, 6" groundcover.			•	•		M	•	•		•			•	•	•			ALL	TS28,39 GC13 AB7
P23 *Erysimum linifolium 'Bowles Mauve'*—Wallflower. One of the most dependable of flowering perennials. The narrow 1-1/2" gray-green leaves lightly cover the 2-1/2" tall rounded form. Lavender flowers on 6" stalks emerge above the shrub in masses in spring, then occasionally through fall. Use as for Golden Shrub Daisy.			•	•		F	•			•	•		•	•		•		14-24	T15,32 TS66 SS7,8 V3,9 GC32,33,34 P14,20 AB1,3 B8,17
P24 *Euphorbia characias wulfenii*—Spurge. Stiff upright blue gray stems are clothed in 1-1/2" blue-gray leaves. Many stems combine to form a 2-1/2 to 3' dome topped by clusters of chartreuse flowers in late winter. Cut to the ground in May.	•		•			M	•				•	•		•	•	•		14-24	T39,54 TS57 SS1,6 V14 OG2 GC17,19 P3,22 AB13 B10

P19
Monkey
Flower

P20
Fortnight
Lily

P21
Fleabane

P22
Siberian
Wallflower

P23
Wallflower

P24
Spurge

Perennials

	Important Characteristics					Cultural Preferences				Tolerances								Aesthetic and Cultural Compatibility
Plant name and description	Deciduous	Evergreen	Flowers	Fall Color	Fruit	Growth Rate	Well Drained Soil	Part Shade	Full Sun	No Water After 2nd Yr.	Monthly Irrigation	Alkaline Soil	Seacoast Conditions	Sprinklers	Wind	Heat	Sunset Zones	
P25 *Gaillardia grandiflora*—Blanket Flower Perennial to 2-4' high. Daisylike flower heads 3-4" across. Ray petals are red to yellow with bands of orange or maroon. Disc petals are usually bronze or maroon. Shorter, bushier forms are available. 'Goblin' is to 6" tall, 18" spread.	●		●			M	●			●						●	ALL	TS1 P44 AB13
P26 *Geranium incanum*—Cranesbill A billowy carpet of fine-textured green foliage, covered with white hairs on the undersides. Rose-purple 1" single flowers cover the plant in spring, with some scattered over it through the summer. Needs semimonthly watering.		●	●			F	●	●	●	●			●		●		● 14-24	TS24,25,42 SS7,8 GC2 P6 AB13
P27 *Geranium sanguineum*—Trailing Geranium Rounded, deeply cut 2" leaves lightly cover the 18" tall, 2' broad trailing stems. Deep purple to red 1-1/2" flowers appear from May through August. Foliage turns blood red in fall. *G.s. prostratum* is lower, compact with pink flowers.	●		●		●	F	●	●	●	●							ALL	T47,61 TS1,8,10 SS2,5 V14 GC25,33 P21,26 AB16 B4
P28 *Hemerocallis species*—Daylilies Above clumps of swordlike 18" to 24" leaves, the clusters of 4-6" diameter flowers are borne on stiff stems. They may be orange, yellow, maroon. 'Hyperion' is heavy, long blooming, with fragrant yellow-orange flowers. Dwarf cultivars with standard size or miniature flowers are available.	●		●	●		M	●	●		●	●	●	●			●	ALL	T13 GC31 P4,5,46
P29 CN *Iris douglasiana and hybrids*—Douglas Iris Clumps of evergreen, 1' to 1-1/2' grass-like leaves. *I. douglasiana* has large green, glossy foliage; flowers in shades of blue. Flowers of hybrids are white, cream, yellow, lavender-blue, to reddish-purple on 1' to 2' stalks. Avoid getting soil in the crown of the plant. Resents sprinklers. Excellent under old oaks.		●	●			S	●	●	●					●	●	●	● 4-24	T53,55 TS70,71 GC28 P20
P30 *Iris foetidissima*—Gladwin Iris Upright 18" tall, 2" broad, dark green leaves form clumps in deep shade or part sun. The gray flowers spotted with chartreuse are not attractive but are followed in late summer with stalked 4" corncobs of brilliant orange 1/2" fruit.		●	●	●		M	●			●			●	●		●	● ALL	T41,46 TS3,32,51 SS13,17 OG1 GC13 P1,8 AB18 B5

P25
Blanket
Flower

P26
Cranesbill

P27
Trailing
Geranium

P28
Daylilies

P29
Douglas Iris

P30
Gladwin
Iris

Perennials

Plant name and description	Deciduous	Evergreen	Flowers	Fall Color	Fruit	Growth Rate	Full Sun	Part Shade	Well Drained Soil	Monthly Irrigation	No Water After 2nd Yr	Seacoast Conditions	Alkaline Soil	Sprinklers	Wind	Heat	Sunset Zones	Aesthetic and Cultural Compatibility
P31 *Iris hybrids*—Bearded Iris The most commonly seen Iris, surviving with no care, but flowering more and longer with semi-weekly water in spring, when the strong 2-4' stalks begin to produce 3-5" flowers in all imaginable colors but red. Cut spent flower stalks. Mix with other plants to hide foliage in summer.	•		•			S	•			•		• •		• •		•	ALL	T38, 57 TS10-14,40 SS7,8 OG2 GC1 P2,4,10 AB1,9 B7
P32 *Kniphofia uvaria*—Red Hot Poker Grasslike 2-4' leaves form a clump from which stalks grow to 3-6' tall, topped by 12" long, full clusters of drooping tubular red, orange or yellow flowers. Too coarse, untidy for foreground. Use in background masses.		•	•			M-F	•	•				• •	•	•			1-9 14-17	GC6,20 P28
P33 *Lantana montevidensis*—Trailing Lantana Slightly hairy dark green 1" leaves, forming tangled mats to 12" high, 3-6' spread. The lilac-colored flowers are borne in 1-1/2" clusters all summer, producing a mat of color. Shear and fertilize in June to keep neat and full. May freeze in zones 14 or 15. Black berries are slightly poisonous.		•	•			F	•		• •	•		•		•		•	15-24	P34, 36,42, 44 AB13
P34 *Lavandula angustifolia, dentata*—English, French Lavender Forms a medium clump about 3' tall. *L. angustifolia* (English Lavender) has lavender bloom July, August, with gray foliage. 'Munstead Dwarf' is 18" with dark lavender flowers. *L. dentata* (French Lavender) has narrow toothed gray-green foliage, blooms almost continuously, and is more tolerant of poor drainage.		•	•			M	•		•			• • •		•			8,9 12-24	T37,51 S14,30,32, 45,48 GC6,29,30 P2,6
P35 *Liatris spicata*—Gay Feather Narrow, grassy 2' foliage is produced by a tuberous root. Three to four tall flower stalks are topped by 16" long flower spikes of lavender-pink 1/2" flowers. The long stalks make good cut flowers.	•		•			F	•		• •					•			1-3 7-10 14-24	T57,61 TS43 SS6 OG5 GC15 P9 AB10 B4
P36 *Limonium perezii*—Sea Lavender The rich, green leaves are a basal cluster of 6" almost round form. Begins producing broad flower clusters up to 3' tall and as wide in summer. The rich purple flowers may remain attractive year round. Good dried flowers.		•	•			F	• • • •		• •	• •		• • • •	•	•			16,17 20-24	T6,7 GC29 P33,43,60

P31
Bearded Iris

P33
Trailing
Lantana

P34
English
Lavender

P35
Gay
Feather

P36
Sea
Lavender

	Important Characteristics						Cultural Preferences			Tolerances							Sunset Zones	Aesthetic and Cultural Compatibility
Plant name and description	Deciduous	Evergreen	Flowers	Fall Color	Fruit	Growth Rate	Well Drained Soil	Part Shade	Full Sun	No Water After 2nd Yr.	Monthly Irrigation	Alkaline Soil	Seacoast Conditions	Sprinklers	Wind	Heat		
P37 Mirabilis jalapa—Four O'Clock A shrubby perennial sown from seeds in spring. They form clumps of dark green leaves to 3' tall topped from summer to fall with red, yellow or white trumpet shaped 2" wide flowers. Plants die to ground in winter, appear again in spring from same roots. Flowers close when sun is off them.	•		•			F			•			•	•	•	•	•	4-14	TS46 SS1 GC32 P46,55 AB3
P38 Myosotis sylvatica—Forget-Me-Not To 6-12" tall, will become a rampant annual ground cover in partial shade. Hairy 1-1/2" leaves cover the bases of the stems while 1/3" clear blue, white-eyed flowers cover the upper stems from late winter to late spring.	•	•	•	•	•	M	•	•	•	•	•	•	•	•	•	•	ALL	TS49 SS1 GC13 AB13 B8,11
P39 Nepeta faassenii—Catmint Soft mounds to 2' high are covered by 1" toothed gray-green leaves. These are topped by shoots of 1/2" lavender-blue flowers in June-July. Shear these off when spent to encourage another bloom and healthier foliage. Use as informal hedge.			•	•		M	•	•						•	•	•	ALL	T43 TS24,25,41 SS5,18 OG1,6 GC24,30 P10,11 AB13 B9
P40 Origanum dictamnus—Dittany of Crete Slender, arching stems to 1' long with evenly spaced 3/4" woolly, silver leaves make a perfect "eyebrow" for topping a rock wall. Flowers like 1" pine cones of chartreuse, pink or lavender, depending on cultivar used, from summer to fall.			•	•		S	•	•	•			•		•	•	•	8-24	T38,48 TS24,52 SS2,4 OG5 GC13,31 P26 AB10 B9,12
P41 Pelargonium hortorum—Common Geranium Shrubby perennial to 3'. Flowers on stalked clusters of white, pink, red, orange. Rounded, 4" leaves are velvety, usually with a band of maroon. Should be pinched semi-monthly to keep neat. Freeze damage may occur at 26°F.			•	•		M	•	•	•					•	•	•	15-17 22-24	GC6,29 P20,49
P42 CN Penstemon heterophyllus purdyi—Beard Tongue Perennial, forming an 8" to 24" tall clump of vertical stems and dark green 1-1/2" leaves. The brilliant blue tubular flowers are borne on spikes from April to July.	•		•			F	•	•	•	•				•	•	•	6-24	T8 GC2,9 P7,11

P37
Four
O'Clock

P38
Forget-
Me-Not

P39
Catmint

P40
Dittany of
Crete

P41
Common
Geranium

P42
Beard
Tongue

110

Perennials

	Important Characteristics					Cultural Preferences			Tolerances									Aesthetic and Cultural Compatibility
Plant name and description	Deciduous	Evergreen	Flowers	Fall Color	Fruit	Growth Rate	Full Sun	Part Shade	Well Drained Soil	Monthly Irrigation	No Water After 2nd Yr.	Alkaline Soil	Seacoast Conditions	Sprinklers	Wind	Heat	Sunset Zones	
P43 CN *Romneya coulteri*—Matilija Poppy	•		•			S-F	•	•		•	•				•	•	12-24	TS23-25,69 GC1,6,29, 30 P44,49,57, 60
P44 *Rudbeckia hirta*—Gloriosa Daisy	•		•			F	•	•				•		•	•	•	ALL	P2,11,22, 50,55
P45 *Ruta graveolens*—Common Rue		•				S	•	•					•	•	•	•	ALL	T20,22 TS24,25,32 SS2,4 V13 OG2,5 GC2,12,13 P2,3,18 AB2,3,10 B1
P46 CN *Salvia clevelandii*—Cleveland Sage		•	•			F	•	•				•			•	•	10-24	TS11,12,14 GC6,11 P43,48,49, 60
P47 *Salvia greggii*—Autumn Sage		•	•			F	•	•						•		•	8-24	T4 TS22,34 SS3,9 V12 OG1,5 GC16,31 P6 AB7 B8,9
P48 *Salvia leucantha*—Mexican Sage		•	•			F	•	•				•				•	10-24	T8 GC31 P19,46,55, 57

P43 — Romneya coulteri—Matilija Poppy

An invasive but spectacular plant, with gray-blue, lobed 3" to 6" leaves on stiff, upright 6-8' stems. Flowers are 6" to 8" wide, with 5 petals like pure white crepe paper. The center is a 2" mound of gold stamens. May bloom from May to July.

P44 — Rudbeckia hirta—Gloriosa Daisy

Stiff flower stalks of 3' to 4', bearing 4" single or double brilliant daisies of golden yellow, orange or mahogany are borne out of a 2' high clump of dark green hairy leaves. Flowering July to October. 'Marmalade' at 18-24" tall is superior.

P45 — Ruta graveolens—Common Rue

The fern-like blue-green foliage forms a dense globe to 2" tall. 'Jackman's Blue' is more compact, silver blue. Its startling color is a good foil for other lavender or yellow flowering plants.

P46 — Salvia clevelandii—Cleveland Sage

A 4' tall, semi-open shrub of aromatic, gray-green 1-1/2' rough leaves. 'Aromas' has brilliant, blue-violet flowers from May to August. Much better with monthly watering. Prune below old flower clusters in June to prolong flowering.

P47 — Salvia greggii—Autumn Sage

An upright, open branched plant to 4 or 6' tall, bearing 1" long rosy-red flowers in loose clusters from June through September. May be sheared into a hedge. Pink and salmon flowered forms also available.

P48 — Salvia leucantha—Mexican Sage

The unbranched 3' to 4' stems lean towards the light. The top 18" is covered with velvety purple flowers during summer and fall, in striking contrast to the gray-green foliage. Cut old stems to ground in winter.

P43
Matilija
Poppy

P44
Gloriosa
Daisy

P45
Common
Rue

P46
Cleveland
Sage

P47
Autumn
Sage

P48
Mexican
Sage

112

Perennials

Plant name and description	Important Characteristics				Cultural Preferences			Tolerances									Aesthetic and Cultural Compatibility
	Evergreen / Deciduous	Flowers	Fall Color	Fruit	Growth Rate	Full Sun	Part Shade	Well Drained Soil	Monthly Irrigation	No Water After 2nd Yr.	Alkaline Soil	Seacoast Conditions	Sprinklers	Wind	Heat	Sunset Zones	
P49 *Santolina chamaecyparissus*—Gray Lavender Cotton		●	●		M-F	●		●	●	●		●	●	●	●	ALL	TS9,11,12, 14 P46,48 GC6,8,9
P50 *Santolina virens*—Green Lavender Cotton		●	●		F	●		●	●	●		●	●	●	●	ALL	TS2 P2-5,37,44 GC2
P51 *Scabiosa columbaria anthemifolia*—Pincushion Flower		●	●		M	●			●				●	●		4-24	T30,62 TS8,24 SS10 V5 OG2,6 GC13 P7,10 AB13 B10,12
P52 *Sedum acre*—Goldenmoss Sedum		●	●		S	●	●		●		●		●	●	●	ALL	T24,25 TS26,36 SS1,15 V7,8 OG6 GC14,30 P18,19 B10
P53 *Sedum sieboldii*	●		●		S	●	●		●				●	●	●	ALL	T9,12 TS20 SS15,18 V17 OG1 GC2,12 P20,31 AB4 B13
P54 CN *Sedum spathulifolium*		●	●		S	●	●	●	●		●	●	●	●	●	ALL	GC2,5,30 P7

P49 *Santolina chamaecyparissus*—Gray Lavender Cotton

Can be 2' tall, 4' spread, but best sheared in March to 1' tall to keep it neat. The whitish-gray 1/2" leaves thickly cover the mounding habit. Buttonlike yellow flowers appear in May-June. *S.c. compacta* is a superior form.

P50 *Santolina virens*—Green Lavender Cotton

A bright green, fine-textured mound of thin twigs to 2' tall, 4' spread. If unpruned, whole foliage mass falls over, producing a leaning plant. Prune heavily after bloom to remove the cream-colored button flowers. Used for its billowy green mass.

P51 *Scabiosa columbaria anthemifolia*—Pincushion Flower

An upright branching plant to 2-1/2' tall, covered with finely dissected, gray-green leaves. The lavender pink 2" flower heads are borne on 2' long stalks from July till fall. Good cut flowers.

P52 *Sedum acre*—Goldenmoss Sedum

In hot sites 3/4" tall creeping, groundcover. Good for use between stepping stones. One-eighth inch, light green leaves fully cover the ground. Tiny clusters of yellow flowers are spotted over the planting in spring. May be invasive in mixed plantings.

P53 *Sedum sieboldii*

The trailing 9" long stems are covered with nickle-sized blue-gray leaves, tipped in red. Each stem produces a flat cluster of dusty pink flowers in October, after which the whole plant turns coppery-red and dies to the ground until spring.

P54 CN *Sedum spathulifolium*

Blue-green 1" rosettes of almost round leaves on trailing stems. To 4" tall with the light yellow flowers appearing above in small clusters in spring-summer. *S. s. purpureum* has deep purple leaves. Small scale groundcover.

P49
Gray
Lavender
Cotton

P50
Green
Lavender
Cotton

P51
Pincushion
Flower

P52
Goldenmoss
Sedum

P53
Sedum
sieboldii

P54
Sedum
spathulifo-
lium

114

Perennials

Plant name and description	Important Characteristics					Cultural Preferences			Tolerances								Sunset Zones	Aesthetic and Cultural Compatibility
	Deciduous	Evergreen	Flowers	Fall Color	Fruit	Growth Rate	Full Sun	Part Shade	Well Drained Soil	Monthly Irrigation	No Water After 2nd Yr.	Alkaline Soil	Seacoast Conditions	Sprinklers	Wind	Heat		
P55 *Senecio cineraria*—Dusty Miller A perennial 2' to 2-1/2' tall, 4' broad. Woolly, white, dissected leaves. Flowers stand above the plant like small yellow thistles. Should be sheared occasionally to keep it neat.		•	•			M	•	•					•		•	•	all but 1-3	T24 TS40 P28,34,36
P56 *Tagetes lemmonii*—Bush Marigold Finely divided foliage is scattered over the semi-open 4' tall shrub. When brushed against, strong aromatic oils are released. The lacy upright structure is covered with golden 1" marigolds from winter through spring. Easily sheared if frost damaged.		•	•			F	•					•		•	•	•	8-10 12-24	T18,20 TS48,53 SS7,8 V3 OG3 GC6,26 P37 AB17 B4
P57 *Teucrium fruticans*—Bush Germander Silvery-gray shrub 4-8' tall and as wide. Narrow 1" leaves are gray-green above, silver underneath. Small lavender-blue flowers in spikes visible most of the year. Spring shearing annually maintains a neat shape.		•	•			F	•	•			•	•		•	•	•	4-24	TS11-14 SS18 GC8-11,20 P42
P58 *Tulbaghia violacea*—Society Garlic Twelve inch bluish-green, grass-like leaves have an onion odor if cut. Flowers are clusters of 10 on 18" stems in rosy lavender, like a miniature *Agapanthus*. Evergreen in mild winters, killed at 20°F. White striped leafed form is most common.		•	•			S	•	•		•		•	•	•	•	•	13-24	T31 TS11,28 SS17 OG2 GC2,15 P36 AB16 B8,9
P59 *Verbena species*—Hybrid Verbena All need sun and heat. Sprinklers create mildew on foliage. *Verbena peruviana, Verbena hybrida* annuals in zones 14, 15, perennial in zones 16, 17. Blue, red or white flower clusters are 1" flattened, brilliant spots against the finely cut green foliage. To 1' tall. Mow in June to prolong flowering.	•		•	•		F	•		•			•		•		•	8-24	T11,55 GC1,6 P55
P60 CN *Zauschneria californica*—California Fuchsia Upright 8-12" stems form a broad mat of gray to gray-green small foliage. Bright orange-red, or white 1-1/2" tubular flowers are borne in clusters at ends of stems from early summer through winter. Invasive if frequently watered. Several selected forms available.	•		•			F	•	•		•		•	•		•	•	14-24	GC29

P55
Dusty
Miller

P57
Bush
Germander

P58
Society
Garlic

P59
Verbena
hybrida

P60
California
Fuchsia

...s and Biennials

Plant name and description	Important Characteristics				Cultural Preferences				Tolerances							Sunset Zones	Aesthetic and Cultural Compatibility
	Evergreen / Deciduous	Flowers	Fall Color	Fruit	Growth Rate	Full Sun	Part Shade	Well Drained Soil	Monthly Irrigation	No Water After 2nd Yr.	Alkaline Soil	Seacoast Conditions	Sprinklers	Wind	Heat		
AB1 *Alcea rosea*—Hollyhock	•	•			F	•			•	•				•	•	ALL	P16 AB3 against garage wall
AB2 *Calendula officinalis*—Calendula	•	•			M	•			•	•					•	ALL	T19,24 AB3,10,13
AB3 *Centaurea cyanus*—Cornflower, Bachelor's Button	•	•			F	•					•		•	•	•	ALL	P2 AB2,10
AB4 *Clarkia species*—Godetia	•	•			M	•	•	•			•				•	ALL	T52-55 TS61 SS2 OG1,5 GC5 P29,34 AB13 B3,7
AB5 *Cleome spinosa*—Spider Flower	•	•			M	•			•		•			•	•	ALL	T38 TS59,61 SS18 V5 GC5,25 P43 B12
AB6 *Coreopsis species*	•	•			F	•			•		•			•	•	ALL	P19,44,60 AB12

AB1 *Alcea rosea*—Hollyhock

A biennial which produces straight stalks up to 8' tall with 4" to 6" single or double flowers distributed along the top 2' of the stem during the summer. Flowers in shades of red, pink, yellow, and white. Spray for Leaf Miner and White Fly.

AB2 *Calendula officinalis*—Calendula

An annual 1' to 2' high, somewhat branching. Orange, yellow, apricot, persimmon, or cream-colored fully double flowers, 2" to 4" across. Blooms late fall to spring in mild areas, spring to mid-summer in colder climates. Install in September to October. Good in hydromulch mix.

AB3 *Centaurea cyanus*—Cornflower, Bachelor's Button

Stiff, 2-1/2' tall stems are topped by brilliant blue, lavender, rose, wine or white frilled 1-1/2" flowers. Sow seed in meadows or flower beds in October.

AB4 *Clarkia species*—Godetia

The upright facing, cup-shaped 2" flowers are the star of the spring show. *C. concinna* to 18" tall, deep lavender flowers. *C. unguiculata* produces 2-3' reddish stems of 1" rose purple flowers. Sow seed in place in fall in sandy soil without fertilizer.

AB5 *Cleome spinosa*—Spider Flower

The 4-6' tall shrubby spined branches are topped in September to November by open clusters of pink or white 2" flowers with long stamens, creating a fluffy effect. A good summer hedge for dry area. Sow seeds in place in warm soil in spring.

AB6 *Coreopsis species*

Annuals and perennials 1' to 3' tall. Most species are upright growing, mass planting subjects, producing quantities of yellow or golden single or double daisylike flowers on long wiry stems, full facing the sun. Most bloom from summer through fall if seed is sown in place in fall.

AB1
Hollyhock

AB2
Calendula

AB3
Bachelor's
Button

AB4
Godetia

AB5
Spider
Flower

AB6
Coreopsis
species

Annuals and Biennials

Plant name and description	Evergreen / Deciduous	Flowers	Fall Color	Fruit	Growth Rate	Full Sun	Part Shade	Well Drained Soil	Monthly Irrigation	No Water After 2nd Yr	Alkaline Soil	Seacoast Conditions	Sprinklers	Wind	Heat	Sunset Zones	Aesthetic and Cultural Compatibility
AB7 *Cosmos bipinnatus 'Dazzler' or 'Radiance'*—Cosmos	●	●			F	●	●		●						●	ALL	GC13 P57 AB13
AB8 *Cosmos sulphureus*—Yellow Cosmos	●	●			F	●		●		●					●	ALL	GC31 P37 AB6
AB9 *Dimorphotheca sinuata*—Cape Marigold	●	●			F	●		●		●			●	●	●	ALL	T10 TS2,15 SS18 OG5 GC12,26 P19
AB10 CN *Eschscholzia californica*—California Poppy	●	●			F	●	●	●		●	●	●		●	●	ALL	T15,20 TS11,12,14 P34 AB3
AB11 *Helianthus annuus*—Sunflower	●	●			F	●			●			●			●	ALL	T49 TS78 SS16 V8,20 OG5 GC31 P2,28 AB9 B10
AB12 *Hunnemannia fumariifolia*—Mexican Tulip Poppy	●	●			M	●	●	●	●						●	ALL	T22,29 TS22,25,28 SS6-8 V13 OG2,3 GC2,8-13 P7,9 AB3,6,10 B12

AB7 — Soft tones of rose, red, or white 3" daisylike flowers, atop 2-4' tall stems from the bright green, fern-like foliage. Flowers appear from summer through fall if old flowers are removed. Best in part shade.

AB8 — May be up to 7' tall in good soil with water in full sun. Branched flower stalks arise from the bright green handsome foliage from summer through fall, if spent flowers are removed. Colors are bright yellow to gold. *'Klondike'* strain blooms earlier at 2-3' tall.

AB9 — Dark green 3" long leaves form an 8" tall cover. Flowers are 1-1/2" orange yellow daisies with violet petal bases appearing during the winter to spring. Flowers close on dull days or in shade. Sow seed in place in early fall in sunny site.

AB10 — Blue-gray, finely dissected foliage to 1' tall, forms a striking background for the shining brilliant orange flowers in early summer. Without water they may be 1-1/2" diameter, with water to 3". If spent flowers are cut off, they can bloom for two months.

AB11 — These 10-12" diameter flower heads are the giants of the annual daisies. Seeds planted in spring will produce 2" diameter, 6-8' tall stalks by late summer, tipped by huge clusters of small flowers, which birds flock to. Smaller flowered, shorter kinds are more useful in the garden, as *'Teddy Bear'*, *'Sungold'*.

AB12 — Blue-green, divided foliage like California Poppy forming a bushy open 2' tall plant which may be perennial in the right condition. Three-inch soft, yellow, cup-shaped flowers appear in July to October. Available in containers.

AB7
Cosmos

AB8
Yellow
Cosmos

AB9
Cape
Marigold

AB10
California
Poppy

AB11
Sunflower

AB12
Mexican
Tulip
Poppy

120

Annuals and Biennials

	Important Characteristics				Cultural Preferences				Tolerances							Sunset Zones	Aesthetic and Cultural Compatibility
Plant name and description	Deciduous / Evergreen	Flowers	Fall Color	Fruit	Growth Rate	Full Sun	Part Shade	Well Drained Soil	Monthly Irrigation	No Water After 2nd Yr.	Alkaline Soil	Seacoast Conditions	Sprinklers	Wind	Heat		
AB13 *Lobularia maritima*—Sweet Alyssum	●	●			F	●	●		● ●	●	●	●	●			14-24	SS8 GC13,30 P46,48 B all
AB14 *Nigella damascena*—Love-in-a-Mist	●	● ●			F	●	●			●					●	ALL	T31 TS51 SS10 V18 OG5 GC12,13 P11,12 AB9 B12
AB15 *Portulaca grandiflora*—Rose Moss	●	●			F	●		●				●		●	● ●	ALL	P49,50 AB3,8,12
AB16 *Scabiosa atropurpurea*—Pincushion Flower	●	●			F	●		●		●		●	●		●	ALL	T33 TS52 SS18 OG4 GC16 P21 AB7 B12
AB17 *Tithonia speciosa*—Torch Flower	●	●			F	●			●			●		●	●	ALL	T63 TS57 SS11 OG3 GC17 P1,25 AB3
AB18 *Tropaeolum majus*—Garden Nasturtium	●	●			VF	● ●		●		●		●		●	● ●	14-24	GC6 P28,55

AB13 *Lobularia maritima*—Sweet Alyssum

A dependable border-edging plant or bulb cover. *'Carpet of Snow'* 4" tall; *'Tiny Tim'* 3" dense habit, bright white flowers; *'Rosie O'Day'* to 4", pink; *'Violet Queen'* to 5" rich purple flowers in summer. May reseed. Shear off spent flowers in June, August to prolong flowering.

AB14 *Nigella damascena*—Love-in-a-Mist

Upright stems, thinly covered with lace-like, thin foliage of gray green branches. To 18-24" tall in 6-8 weeks in spring or summer, depending upon seed sowing date. Light to medium blue (or white) 1-1/2" flowers appear profusely over ends of branches, followed by attractive 1-1/2" 'paper lantern' seed capsules.

AB15 *Portulaca grandiflora*—Rose Moss

One inch long, cylindrical, succulent leaves are borne along the trailing stems, forming a full mat of bright green. Flowers like 1-1/2" roses cover the plant with a kaleidoscope of all the warm colors from July until frost. Flowers open only in full sun. Plant from flats in spring.

AB16 *Scabiosa atropurpurea*—Pincushion Flower

A 2-1/2" upright branching bush with deeply toothed green foliage. The pincushion-like summer flowers are in 2" dense clusters on 2' wiry stems which are good as cut flowers. Colors from deep purple to pink or white. May be purchased in flats. Can reseed into garden.

AB17 *Tithonia speciosa*—Torch Flower

Plants installed from flats in early spring become 4' tall stalks with brilliant orange 4" flowers with yellow centers. Use in a background where lower stems are hidden. Excellent cut flowers, if stems are not bent when collecting.

AB18 *Tropaeolum majus*—Garden Nasturtium

An annual in zones 14, 15, 16, perennial in zone 17, where it may naturalize as a floriferous bank cover. Three inch round, lush leaves are the background for the 2" edible, tubular flowers with a nectar filled "tail". Shrubby or climbing forms in mixed or single colors of yellow, orange or mahogany are available.

AB13
Sweet
Alyssum

AB14
Love-in-a-
Mist

AB15
Rose Moss

AB16
Pincushion
Flower

AB17
Torch
Flower

AB18
Garden
Nasturtium

122

Bulbs

Plant name and description

	Deciduous	Evergreen	Flowers	Fall Color	Fruit	Growth Rate	Full Sun	Part Shade	Well Drained Soil	Monthly Irrigation	No Water After 2nd Yr.	Alkaline Soil	Seacoast Conditions	Sprinklers	Wind	Heat	Sunset Zones	Aesthetic and Cultural Compatibility
B1 *Alstroemeria ligtu hybrids*—Peruvian Lily	●		●			M	●		●	●	●			●	●	●	5-9 14-16 24	T38,54 TS11-14 SS5-18 OG5 GC2,3,8-10
B2 *Amaryllis belladonna*—Naked Lady Lily	●		●			M	●	●	●				●	●	●	●	4-24	T8 AB3 B2
B3 *Anemone blanda*	●		●			S	●	●				●				●	1-9 4-23	T38,52-55 TS29,30 SS6,17 OG1 GC2,3 B7
B4 *Crocosmia crocosmiiflora*—Montbretia	●		●			F	●					●	●	●	●	●	5-24	P4,11,55
B5 *Cyclamen hederifolium*	●		●			S		●		●		●				●	1-9 14-23	T38,52-55 TS29 SS2,3,18 OG1 GC2 B8
B6 *Freesia Tecolote Hybrids*	●		●			F	●	●				●	●	●	●	●	8,9 12-24	T8,9 TS8 SS1 OG1 GC26

B1 — Stiff, vertical stems appear from the ground in late winter to bloom May-July. Flowers of 2" yellow, pink, orange-red and lilac are loose clusters atop the 2' to 4' stems. Very invasive. Remove seed pods to help control. Water frequently in spring. New hybrids have larger flowers in more colors and are less invasive.

B2 — This bulb produces clumps of 2' to 3' straplike leaves which appear in winter and disappear by early summer. Clusters of 6" rosy pink trumpets on 2' reddish-brown stalks appear out of bare ground in August. May not bloom two to three years after transplanting.

B3 — Planted as tuberous roots in fall, the finely divided green leaves appear in spring, forming a light cover 3" high. This is followed in April by sky-blue, white or pink 1-1/2" daisy-like flowers. Use with other small-scale plants or in rock garden.

B4 — Sword-shaped leaves to 3' tall in clumps. In summer 3' to 4' branched flower stems produce 1-1/2" orange or orange-red flowers for 30 days. Use in perimeter areas; can be invasive. *C. masoniorum* has orange-scarlet flowers. Both are excellent cut flowers.

B5 — Tubers set at 1/2 of their depth in well-drained soil in a flower bed or in pots will produce 3" heart-shaped, marbled silver leaves in spring, followed by 1/2" rose-pink, miniature Cyclamen. Must be dry in summer, so good for use under oaks.

B6 — Branched 12" stems of 2" tubular flowers are borne above the 8" iris-like foliage in early spring in any color of the rainbow. Seedlings may revert to the cream-colored flowers with purple markings of the species. Intensely fragrant and excellent as cut flowers.

B1
Peruvian
Lily

B2
Naked
Lady Lily

B3
Anemone
blanda

B4
Montbretia

B5
Cyclamen
hederifolium

B6
Freesia
Tecolote
Hybrids

Bulbs

Plant name and description	Important Characteristics				Cultural Preferences				Tolerances							Sunset Zones	Aesthetic and Cultural Compatibility
	Evergreen/Deciduous	Flowers	Fall Color	Fruit	Growth Rate	Well Drained Soil	Part Shade	Full Sun	No Water After 2nd Yr	Monthly Irrigation	Seacoast Conditions	Alkaline Soil	Sprinklers	Wind	Heat		
B7 *Narcissus*—Daffodil Bulbs which produce trumpet shaped flowers in shades of yellow, orange, buff and white in spring. Clumps with narrow, straplike foliage expand over many years without care. Gophers and most insects ignore them. Various cultivars bloom from December–March.	•	•			F	•	•						•	•	•	ALL	T8 GC29 P4
B8 *Scilla peruviana*—Peruvian Scilla Straplike 8" to 12" dark green leaves appear in winter. In April–May, 10" to 12" stalks bear 5" diameter domes of blue-purple star-like flowers. Leaves die down after bloom. Will grow in deep shade or hot sun. Best colors are produced in dappled shade.	•	•			F	•	•	•	•	•			•		•	14-17 19-24	T14 B11
B9 *Tulipa clusiana*—Lady Tulip Red and white candy striped 2" long buds in early spring open to 2" wide flowers. Cut the 9" tall stems with buds for long lasting cut flowers. Lady Tulip will slowly reproduce to form a large colony in well-drained soil. Attractive to gophers.	•	•			M	•	•									ALL	T8,9 TS22 SS2 OG2 GC30,31 B7
B10 *Watsonia pyramidata*—Watsonia Robust 5' flower stems rise out of the clump of 3' New Zealand Flax-like leaves in late spring. Clusters of rose-pink, rose-red or white 2" flowers begin opening midway up the stalk and appear over a month.	•	•			F	•							•	•		4-9 12-24	T15 TS54 SS18 OG5 GC20 P14,15 AB13
B11 *Zantedeschia aethiopica*—Calla Lilly Basal clumps of 12" lance-shaped leaves on 18" stems appear in later winter, die down after blooming unless regularly watered. Flowers are really 8" broad, pure white bracts wrapped around the spike of tiny yellow true flowers. Excellent for naturalizing, especially in wet spots. Excellent cut flowers and foliage. Other species with yellow or pink flowers.	•	•			S	•	•						•		•	14-24	TS43 B8
B12 *Zephyranthes candida*—Zephyr Flower Bright green, glossy evergreen clumps of grass-like 12" foliage is topped by 2" pure white Crocus-like flowers from summer through fall. Plant in full sun or part shade in well-drained soil. Flowers longer with occasional irrigation.		•			M	•	•	•							•	1-9 14-24	T1,15 TS2,29 SS2,18 GC1,15 P22,33

B7
Daffodil

B8
Peruvian
Scilla

B9
Lady Tulip

B10
Watsonia

B11
Calla Lilly

B12
Zephyr
Flower

Ferns
and Fernlike Plants

Plant name and description	Evergreen / Deciduous	Flowers	Fall Color	Fruit	Growth Rate	Full Sun	Part Shade	Well Drained Soil	Monthly Irrigation	No Water After 2nd Yr.	Alkaline Soil	Seacoast Conditions	Sprinklers	Wind	Heat	Sunset Zones	Aesthetic and Cultural Compatibility
F1 **Asparagus densiflorus 'Sprengeri'—Sprenger Asparagus**	●				M	●	●	●					●	●	●	12-24	T16,17,61 TS26,46 SS1,14
F2 **Cyrtomium falcatum—Holly Fern**	●				S-M		●	●						●	●	15-17	T53,62 TS49,50,72, 76 SS14 GC28
F3 **Davallia trichomanoides—Squirrel's Foot Fern**	●				S	●	●	●							●	16-17	T49,62,65 TS49,72,76 SS14 GC28 P8
F4 **Dryopteris erythrosora—Autumn Fern**	●				S-M		●	●							●	ALL	T38,53 TS49,72,76 SS14 GC28 P8
F5 **Nephrolepis cordifolia—Southern Sword Fern**	●				M		●	●					●	●	●	16-17	T53,62 TS49,71,72, 76 SS14 P8
F6 CN **Polystichum munitum—Western Sword Fern**	●				M		●	●					●	●	●	ALL	T53,62 TS49,.72,76 SS14 GC28 P8

F1 Not a true fern, but often used as one. It makes a good ground cover in semishaded areas (above 24°F). The bright green 1" needlelike leaves clothe the arching 1' stems to form "plumes" of foliage. Must have well-drained soil and fertilizer.

F2 Two to 3' tall, coarse-textured, dark green, leathery foliage needs once per month deep watering. Do not plant deeper than soil level in container. Good background for other ferns.

F3 Once established in shade in a well-drained soil, this lacy textured fern will survive with bimonthly watering. Bright green 12" fronds arise from fuzzy brown surface roots. Use as a ground cover. Tender at 28°F.

F4 Used in shade or filtered shade, the young fronds are reddish bronze, maturing to 2' fronds of deep green in late spring. Excellent for use under trees.

F5 Bright green fronds to 2' to 3' tall form clumps of vertical form. Spreads by thin runners making new plants. Very resilient. Prune to ground in spring and fertilize.

F6 CN Medium green, 2' fronds in sun, dark green 3' fronds in shade. Arching, graceful form. Best in semishade in any zone, shade only, zones 14-15.

F1
Sprenger
Asparagus

F2
Holly Fern

F3
Squirrel's
Foot Fern

F4
Autumn
Fern

F5
Southern
Sword Fern

F6
Western
Sword
Fern

128

Resources

Water Conserving Landscapes

The East Bay Municipal Utility District (EBMUD) in cooperation with various public agencies, has developed several demonstration water-conserving landscapes in Alameda and Contra Costa Counties. 1991 locations include:

Fire Station, 180 Refugio Valley Rd., Hercules

Fire Station, 331 Rheem Blvd., Moraga

The Resource Garden, Lake Merritt, Oakland

EBMUD Office, 3189 Danville Blvd., Alamo

Heather Farm Garden Center, 1540 Marchbanks Drive, Walnut Creek

Residence, 1376 Rose St., Berkeley

Post Office, 2101 Pear St., Pinole

Call the District's Water Conservation Office at (510) 287-0590 for the location of the newest demonstration garden sites, or for information on materials and services.

Material and Services

Free water conservation material and services available from EBMUD Include:

Publications:
- Water Conservation Material & Services
- Puddlestoppers Handbook
- Waterwise Gardening
- Drip Irrigation Guidelines

Sunset Magazine Reprints:
- Drip (About drip irrigation)
- How Much Water Does Your Lawn Really Need?
- The Unthirsty 100
- 80 Ways to Save Water in the Garden

Video:
- Beautiful Gardens with Less Water (30 minutes)

Equipment:
- Water saving showerheads (2 gallons/minute)
- Water saver kit (2 plastic water displacement bags and 2 dye tablets to detect toilet leaks)
- Moisture Meter
- Self-closing hose nozzle

Services:
- Lawn watering information: (510) 820-7750 (CIMIS, 24 hour)
- Indoor and outdoor water audits: (510) 287-0590
- Multi-Family device distribution: (510) 287-0590
- Landscape plan review/consultation: (510) 287-0590

Reference Books

Additional information on drought-tolerant plants can be obtained from the following publications:

Australian Native Plants, J.W. Wrigley and M. Fagg, William Collins Pty, Australia, 1980

Bulbs—How To Select, Grow and Enjoy, G. H. Scott, H.P. Books, Tucson, Arisona 1982

California Native Trees and Shrubs, L. Leenz and J. Dourley, Rancho Santa Ana Botanic Garden, Claremont, CA 1981

Gardening in Dry Climates, Ortho Books, Santa Barbara, CA 1989

Growing California Native Plants, M.G. Schmidt, University of California Press, Berkeley, CA 1980

Lawn and Groundcovers, M. MacCaskey, H.P. Books, Tucson, AZ 1982

Ornamental Grasses—The Amber Wave, C. Ottsen, 1989

Plants for Dry Climates, M.R. Duffield, & W.D. Jones, H.P. Books, Tucson, AZ 1981

Selected Native Plants in Color, B. Coate and D. White, Saratoga Horticultural Foundation, San Martin, CA 1980

Success List of Water Conserving Plants, Saratoga Horticultural Foundation, Saratoga, CA 1983

Sunset Western Garden Book, Lane Publishing Co., Menlo Park,CA 1988

Trees and Shrubs for Dry California Landscapes, B. Perry, Land Design Publishing, San Dimas, CA, 1981

Trees and Shrubs for Temperate Climates, G. Courtright, Timber Press, Beaverton, Oregon, 1988

Waterwise Gardening, Lane Publishing Co., Melno Park, CA1989

Wholesale Nurseries

If you have trouble locating plant material listed in this book, ask your retail nursery to contact a local wholesale nursery or one of the following (All are in California unless otherwise noted.) Those carrying ornamental grasses are noted (OG).

Blue Oak Nursery, 2731 Mountain Oak Lane, Rescue, 95672

Calaveras Nursery, 1622 Hwy. 12, Valley Springs, 95252

California Conservation Corps (Public Projects and Agencies only) P.O. Box 7199, Napa, 94558

California Flora Nursery, P.O. Box 3, Fulton, 95439 (OG)

California Native Plant Society, Merritt College, Oakland, (OG)

Christensen Nursery Company, 935 Old County Road, Belmont, 94002

Circuit Riders Productions (contract growing) 9619 Old Redwood Hwy., Windsor, 95492

Clotilde Merlo Forest Nursery, Louisiana-Pacific Corporation, Trinidad, 95570

D.A.W.N., Berkeley Marina (Spinnaker Way by Berths A-E), Berkeley (OG)

Elfinwood Nursery, 405 Sylvan Rd., Colfax, 95713

Forestfarm, 990 Tetherow Road, Williams, OR 97544

G & N Native Plant Nursery, 164 Panoramic Way, Walnut Creek, 94595

Greener 'N' Ever Tree Farm and Nursery, P.O. Box 222435, Carmel, 93922

Greenlee Nursery, 301 E. Franklin Ave., Pomona, 91766 (OG only)

H & H Forest Tree Nursery, P.O. Box 479, Sebastopol, 95472

Heritage Garden Growers Inc., Box 7184, Menlo Park, 94026

Las Pilitas Nursery, Star Route Box 23X, Santa Margarita, 93453

Mostly Natives Nursery, P.O. Box 226, 27215 Hwy. 1 (at 2nd St.), Tomales, 94971 (OG)

The Native Nursery, P.O. Box 1684, Big Bear City, 92314

Native Sons Wholesale Nursery, 379 West El Camp Road, Arroyo Grande, 93420

Oki Nursery Co., P.O. Box 7118, Sacramento, 95828

Pacific Nurseries of California, 2099 Hillside Boulevard, Colma, 94014

San Marcos Growers, 125 S. San Marcos Rd., Santa Barbara, 93111

Saratoga Horticultural Foundation, 15185 Murphy Avenue, San Martin, 95046

Shooting Star Propagation, 9950 O'Connell Road, Sebastopol, 95472

Skylark Wholesale Nursery, 6735 Sonoma Highway, Santa Rosa, 95405 (OG)

Stribling's Nurseries, Inc., P.O. Box 793, 6529 Mariposa Way, Merced, 95340

Theodore Payne Foundation, 10459 Tuxford St., Sun Valley, 91352

Tiedemann Nursery, 4835 Cherryvale Avenue, Soquel, 95073

Tree of Life, P.O. Box 736, San Juan Capistrano, 92693

Valley Crest Tree Company, 13745 Sayre St., Sylmar, 91342

Wapumne Native Plant Nursery Co., 8305 Cedar Crest Way, Sacramento, 95826

Western Hills Nursery, 16250 Coleman Valley Rd., Occidental, 95465 (OG)

Western Tree Nursery, 3280 Hecker Pass Highway, Gilroy, 95020

Wildwood Farm, 10300 Highway 12, Kenwood, 95452

Wintergreen Nursery, 358 Merk Rd., Watsonville, 95076

Ya-Ka-Ama Indian Education Center, 6215 Eastside Road, Forestville, 95436

Yerba Buena Nursery, 19500 Skyline Boulevard, Woodside, 94062 (OG)

Zenny's Native Plants, 76 Howell Lane, Corralitos, 95076

Seed Companies (Grasses, Wildflowers, Hydroseed)

Albright Seed Company (G), 487 Dawson Dr., 5-S, Camarillo, 93010

Clyde Robin Seed Co., 25670 Nickel Place, Hayward, 94545

Conservaseed (G), P.O. Box 455, Rio Vista, 94571

Environmental Seed Producers, P.O. Box 5904, El Monte, 91734

Larner Seeds, P.O. Box 407, Bolinas, 94924

Moon Mountain Seed, P.O. Box 34, Morro Bay, 93442

Pacific Coast Seed, Inc., P.O. Box 2908, Dublin, 94568

Wildflowers International, Inc., 918-B Enterprise Way, Napa, 94556

Bibliography

All About Tall Fescue, A. Harivandi, University of California Cooperative Extension in Alameda County, 1982

A California Flora and Supplement, P. Munz and D. Keck, University of California Press, Berkeley, CA 1968

Descriptive Catalog of Ornamental Grasses, J. Greenlee, Pomona, CA 1987

A Guide to Erosion Control in Santa Cruz County, Watershed Management Office, County of Santa Cruz, 1977

Hard Fescue for Minimum Maintenance, A. Harivandi, University of California Cooperative Extension in Alameda County, 1982

Homeowners' Guide to Fire and Watershed Management at the Chaparral Urban Interface, USDA, Forest Service and County of Los Angeles, 1982

The Impact of Bans of Watering Landscape Plants, American Association of Nurserymen

Oak Woodland Preservation and Land Planning, N. Hardesty, Portola Valley Ranch, Menlo Park, CA 1983

Plants for California Landscapes, California State Department of Water Resources, 1981

A Success List of Water-Conserving Plants, Saratoga Horticultural Foundation, 1983

Sunset Western Garden Book, Lane Publishing Company, Menlo Park, California, 1988